Praise for

HOW **NOT** TO BE A **HOT MESS**

"Modern life is messy, aggravating, even injurious. Despite this truth, the authors show us how to see the goodness. This book is part of that goodness—transforming the ability to survive into the ability to thrive."

Larry Yang, author of *Awakening Together*

"For Devon and Craig Hase, a clear mind and wise choices are what enable us to define ourselves in a frenetic world. Writing with a combination of wit, refreshing honesty, and wisdom, they give us a guide to reclaiming our true selves from the definitions of the world, so that we can enjoy the happiness this brings."

Sharon Salzberg, author of *Lovingkindness* and *Real Happiness*

"In their excellent first book, Devon and Craig Hase offer a remarkably effective roadmap to living life with greater ease and full integrity. I'm delighted to recommend this new book to absolutely everyone—especially millennials."

Susan Kaiser Greenland, author of *Mindful Games* and *The Mindful Child,* founder of Inner Kids

"*How Not to Be a Hot Mess* by Craig and Devon Hase is an engaging exploration of how to bring dharma practice into the nitty-gritty of our lives. It offers a clear-sighted view of the challenges of these times and the potential for living with integrity and deepening understanding in the midst of them. As its subtitle suggests, it is indeed a survival guide for modern life—a guide written with insight, humor, and great friendliness."

Joseph Goldstein, author of *Mindfulness*

"This book is more 'walk' than 'talk,' though it's backed by serious Buddhist philosophy, scientific research, and personal stories. Mindfulness is just the beginning—if we're still acting like messes or jerks, as if our practice is all about 'me' feeling better, then we probably need to attune more deeply into our innate goodness and make a few changes. In a sweetly humorous tone, Devon and Craig invite us to take a super-serious look at how we live. A long-overdue contribution to the mindfulness conversation."

Kate Lila Wheeler

HOW **NOT**
TO BE A
HOT MESS

HOW NOT TO BE A HOT MESS

A Survival Guide for Modern Life

Craig Hase & Devon Hase

SHAMBHALA
Boulder
2020

SHAMBHALA PUBLICATIONS, INC.
4720 Walnut Street
Boulder, Colorado 80301
www.shambhala.com

9 8 7 6 5 4 3 2 1

First Edition
Printed in the United States of America

♾ This edition is printed on acid-free paper that meets the
American National Standards Institute z39.48 Standard.
♻Shambhala Publications makes every effort to print on recycled paper.
For more information please visit www.shambhala.com.

Shambhala Publications is distributed worldwide by
Penguin Random House, Inc., and its subsidiaries.

Designed by Kate Huber-Parker

LIBRARY OF CONGRESS CATALOGING-IN-PUBLICATION DATA
Names: Hase, Craig, author. | Hase, Devon, author.
Title: How not to be a hot mess: a survival guide for
modern life / Craig Hase and Devon Hase.
Description: First edition. | Boulder: Shambhala, 2020.
Identifiers: LCCN 2019022861 | ISBN 9781611807981 (hardcover)
Subjects: LCSH: Conduct of life. | Buddhism. | Meditation. |
Mindfulness   (Psychology) | Spiritual life.
Classification: LCC BJ1589 .H38 2020 | DDC 158.1/3—dc23
LC record available at https://lccn.loc.gov/2019022861

TO OUR TEACHERS

Lama Pema and Lama Yeshe,
NDR, Zentatsu, Joseph Goldstein
Mingyur Rinpoche, and all the rest

We tried really hard to say everything you said to us,
But in a way our not-so-Buddhist friends
would understand.

Hope we didn't screw it up.

CONTENTS

HOW **NOT**
TO BE A
HOT MESS

INTRODUCTION

There is a story from the Buddhist canon we'd like to share. It has to do with doubt and storms and taking your place in the middle of everything.

In this story, the Buddha is not yet the Buddha. He's a young prince-turned-mendicant named Siddhartha. He has just spent six years meditating, pushing himself to the brink of death in his epic quest for the answer to everything. Now it's the moment right before the tangle of his mind unbinds, the moment before he achieves full, complete awakening and leaves suffering behind for good.

But first things get crazy. Because as he sits down under a tree, as he closes his eyes to meditate one more time on the ultimate nature of things, as he drops deeper and deeper into the concentration that will finally end his quest—a demon appears. And not just any demon, but the demon Mara, who embodies delusion and doubt and obfuscation and who wields untold power over the capricious minds of mortals.

First, Mara sends his daughters to tempt the Buddha-to-be. But Siddhartha is unmoved.

Next, Mara sends armies of terrifying demons to shake the young prince from his seat. But their arrows turn into flowers.

Finally, Mara hits him with a final gambit. "Who are you," he says to the thirty-six-year-old seeker who has abandoned everything in his search for truth, "to think you can sit in this hallowed seat? Who is your witness?"

Siddhartha pauses for a moment. Maybe he even hesitates. Who isn't prone to the sneaky messenger of doubt?

But then, sitting cross-legged in meditation, the young man begins to list for Mara his goodness. He remembers moment after moment of generosity, patience, service—all the instances of standing upright in the middle of the storm. He steadies his mind. He places his hand on the ground. And he says, simply, "The earth is my witness."

Mara is vanquished. The Buddha is awakened. And the rest is history.

Standing Upright in the Storm

Pretty cool, right? But most of us, most of the time, don't have that kind of clarity. That's why this book is for those who are lost in the storm: blinded by the blizzard of information, the hurricane of stimulation, the typhoon of opinions and judgments and how-tos and must-dos. Those who feel, as we all often do, like a phenomenally dysregulated hot mess, one step behind it all, a storm within the storm, lavishly disorganized and exhausted and not-quite-with-it as the world somehow spins on, never quite sitting still while we never quite sit still, either.

This book is for all of us who would like to know exactly just what to do with life in its magnificent rush of pleasure and pain, gain and loss, its dreamlike phantasmagoria of web-based temptations and quasi-demonic forces. It's for all of us who would like to know, too, what to do with our anger, hopelessness, confusion, ideals, ideas, and big questions. How do we settle the hot mess of our own lives, anyway, when the world seems to be spinning off its axis?

That's what this book is about. It draws on Buddhist advice because, believe it or not, Buddhism has been through it all before. It's seen wars, plagues, oppression, and ten thousand terrible haircuts—and it has, along the way, developed dependable ways to stay steady in the roller coaster of family feuds, romantic vacillations, uncertain futures, and all the rest. This book offers six pieces of really good advice drawn from this 2,600-year-old wisdom tradition. These six pieces of really good advice can help you determine just exactly how you can settle the hot mess of your mind and stand in your uprightness smack in the middle of everything. Like the Buddha, when he touched the earth and decided he wasn't going to take Mara's shit anymore.

Mindfulness Is Not Enough

Fine. Sounds good, you might say. Stand upright. Settle the hot mess of my mind. No more shit from Mara. But where do we start?

We start with mindfulness.

Mindfulness has been getting a lot of press these days. And for good reason. Because mindfulness is the very cornerstone of a life well lived. It's the ability to pay stable attention to whatever is happening, right now, in all its weirdness and complexity, without turning away. It's the simple warmhearted awareness of *this*.

So mindfulness is power. Mindfulness is beauty. But there's something you should probably know. Something no one is really talking about. Put simply, all the mindful magazines and mindful business consultants and mindful sex coaches and mindful apps and mindful advertising gurus are missing a great, big, giant, massive, right-in-your-face, glaring kind of problem: mindfulness alone is not enough.[1]

Mindfulness is not enough to live a levelheaded existence right in the middle of the storm that is contemporary life. Mindfulness is not enough to find your way through the cyclone of your days. It's not enough to help you make the tough choices. And here's the real kicker: it was never meant to be enough.

When the Buddha taught mindfulness, he always taught it as part of a whole. He never said, "Pay attention to your breath and you will be free of suffering." More like, "Pay attention to your breath as a way of steadying the mind, and then look at your life."

Look at your life. Closely. Notice your mind states. Notice your heart states. And, also, if you want to be happy, make sure you're really taking care of things. Like goodness, and sweetness, and love, and compassion. In fact, the Buddha said goodness, not mindfulness, is the foundation for a happy life.

Good Is Good

The basic assertion of this book, then, is that good is good. Like, it's good to do good. And it not only *is* good, it also *feels* good. So yes, you should act on all your better urges—you should help the old lady cross the street, give money to charity, say kind things to your friends, and keep your head on straight.

How? Well, in addition to practicing mindfulness—which of course we highly recommend—we'd like to offer five more hot-mess-busting pieces of semi-Buddhist advice. And they are as follows:

1. Don't Be a Jerk
2. Give a Little
3. Say What's True
4. Make Sex Good
5. Stay Clear

In Buddhism, we call these the *precepts*. Think of them as a road map. Or an instruction manual. Don't think of them as rigid prescriptions for how to be some sort of plasticine smiling goody-two-shoes. They're more like trainings. You can just try them out and see what happens. In fact, you can take each one of them with a giant grain of salt. Take one at a time into your days, knock around with it for a while, and see if things get better. Meanwhile, as you try them out and see what happens, you'll likely find that they build on each other, ricochet off one another, and overall end up being a pretty stormproof formula for how to be happy and live a halfway decent existence.

So in the following pages we're going to unpack what it actually takes to live these principles in real time: in the classroom, the boardroom, and the bedroom; in the chatroom and, God help us all, in the comments section of the *Washington Post*. We'll talk about our own failures—maybe some successes, too—we'll tell a bunch of stories, and we'll pepper the whole thing with references to the best psychological literature out there that is looking at how to accomplish the good life.

What we won't do is talk to you about the complexities of Buddhist cosmology. We won't ask you to sign on for yet another belief system. But just know that, in addition to some great studies and our own personal experiences, there is also the time-tested wisdom of the whole of Buddhism that we're trying to pack into this little missive, which carries with it a thousand minds and hearts that have road-tested every one of these principles in their very real, very vulnerable lives. Just like you, these friends—our Buddhist ancestors—have wanted to live a life that is happy, satisfying, and meaningful. They've succeeded. We think you can, too.

One Last Thing

Who the heck are we? Are we greatly enlightened spiritual masters who are going to give you all the answers? Are we here to solve all your problems? Have we even solved all our own problems?

In a word: nope.

We're not great spiritual teachers. We're just two seekers who have tried to put these principles at the center of our lives. They've worked for us. They still are working in us. And while we can't say we're all that realized or all that special, we can say with conviction that we live a life that is, all in all, astonishingly ordinary and very happily adequate.

Yeah, okay, but who are we?

We're a white, hetero, cisgender, middle-class, hyper-educated American couple who have studied with some of the great Asian and American Buddhist teachers alive today. We've been at it for about twenty years each. We've spent years in meditation retreat and years studying old Buddhist books, new Buddhist books, and a small mountain of psychology studies—all in this sometimes bewildering attempt to live an ethical and energized life that will benefit us, we hope, and maybe even benefit others, too.

Craig has a PhD in psychology.

Devon was a classroom teacher for a decade before starting to teach meditation full-time.

We're basically here to pass on what we've learned to you in the hope that it can be immediately applicable in your attempts to survive modern life with your heart and mind intact.

Now let's have some fun.

MEDITATE

Devon

There are approximately one bajillion reasons why you should probably be meditating right now. Leaving aside any particularly Buddhist ones—like enlightenment, or nirvana, or complete liberation from the endless cycle of suffering— there are some totally legit, immediately beneficial ways mindfulness and meditation can be good for you starting *today*. We'll get to the cold, hard facts soon. But first, I wanted to share a bit about how I began.

MY STORY

I was born in an artsy small town in southern Oregon to stable, loving parents. My dad worked with Carl Rogers, the great humanist psychologist, until the late '70s, then got into property management so that he could be a stay-at-home parent with me, the only child. My mom was a California-trained architect obsessed with small-is-beautiful sustainable design.

Things at home were, overall, pretty great. We sang songs at dinner; we rarely fought; we all dressed up for Halloween in matching costumes. Picture a hippie New Age rendition of the Cleavers.

Still, like everybody, I suffered from everyday eviscerations, plagues of self-doubt and anxiety. As a white woman, cisgender and mostly straight, who grew up with a lot of safety and family love and wellness, it's not so easy to talk about the things that were hard for me. I know many of my friends confronted, and still confront, whole other levels of difficulty, from abuse and financial instability to racism and systemic injustice. But even for me, in my sheltered life, I was suffering. Especially starting in my teens, I experienced a growing dread, this gut-tightening drive to be better, happier, thinner, a radiant model of accomplishment and good cheer.

All these perfectionist tendencies led to good things, like being the valedictorian of my high school class and winning an academic scholarship to a semi-exclusive liberal arts college. But slowly the need to be better and different caught up to me. This sense of being squeezed out of myself, out of my own body, grew and grew. And then I got to college, joined a sorority, and kind of lost my mind.

My first semester on campus stands out for me as a blur of under-eating, over-exercising, and trying to make my body into someone else's body (skinnier, tighter, smaller) and my mind into someone else's mind (elated, ever-sunny). I lasted until about Christmas break, maybe four months.

Then, home for the holidays, surrounded by family and friends, I ended up sobbing on my parents' kitchen floor, immobilized by a tidal wave of self-loathing and feelings of utter worthlessness. My mom, ever the pragmatist, gave me a book by Pema Chödrön, the great American Buddhist nun and meditation teacher and effortless communicator of deepest human truths.

Reading Pema Chödrön, it became utterly clear to me what had happened. Slowly, unwittingly, I had bought in: bought in to the cruel and unreasonable images of what a quasi-perfected body should be; bought in to sorority norms of hyper-feminized effervescence; bought in to the whole objectifying patriarchal consumerist imbroglio (see chapter 5). I saw, that night, reading Pema in an old easy chair, that these screwball internalized regulations, these unexamined shoulds and must-dos, were literally wrecking me from the inside out. Not eating when I was hungry, not stopping when I was tired, pushing through and pushing past every healthy boundary in my quest for some far-fetched standard of culturally sanctioned goodness, beautifulness, desirability, I had driven myself into digestive distress, episodes of dizziness and unreality, and a mind spun out on standards I could never fully achieve.

With these realizations, something in me just cracked open. I found something in Pema's words that I had never heard before. It was radical and so simple. The way out, she said, was to get real. And in particular, to sit down and look at my own mind.

So that's what I did. I began meditating. That summer, I went to a young adults' retreat at Spirit Rock Meditation Center. Not long after that, I met my first teachers, two Western women lamas named Pema and Yeshe, who had just completed the traditional Tibetan three-year retreat. Within a year I was absolutely hooked on meditation. Not to mention the slow process of digging myself out of the societal delirium that so many generations of women seem to fall into: namely, thinking that whatever our body is, it should somehow, inexplicably and impossibly, be other, better, and, above all, *less.*

So yes, meditation worked for me. And the more it worked, the more I did it. And the more I did it, the more it worked. And then at some point, in addition to just doing meditation, I eventually started teaching it. This doesn't mean I never get caught up all over again in the dream world of culturally enforced impossible expectations and other delirious forms of suffering. But it does mean that I'm a little better at waking myself up, over and over again, from the dream.

SO WHAT IS MINDFULNESS AND MEDITATION?

The ancient Buddhist word for mindfulness is *sati. Sati,* it turns out, is a richly complex signifier, and its meaning has been debated for centuries. For our purposes, however, we can define *sati* as "awareness." It is the capacity of the mind to know. Awareness knows the five senses, it knows thoughts, it knows feeling tone and emotional valence. And when that capacity to know is developed, we can call it mindfulness. Or, as Jon Kabat-Zinn says, "Mindfulness is the awareness that arises through paying attention on purpose in the present moment—non-judgmentally."[1]

Thousands of research studies have now shown that developing this capacity to know experience with a nonreactive awareness leads to a staggering range of mental and physical health benefits. (We'll get to that soon.)

The ancient Buddhist word for meditation, on the other hand, is *bhavana*. Put simply, bhavana means "cultivation," and in Buddhist literature it refers to any practice that actively develops beneficial mind states. So when meditators are inclining the mind toward concentration, kindness, compassion, or joy, they are engaged in bhavana.

In a nutshell, we can say that *meditation* refers to a broad range of practices designed to help human beings suffer less and live with greater ease and well-being. *Mindfulness* is both the capacity of the mind to know and the development of that capacity. It is both an ingredient in all meditation practices and a type of meditation all by itself.

So throughout this book, we're going to offer some quick meditations. Of course, it's hard to meditate when you're reading. Feel free to slow down and read this meditation once through, and then do it on your own later. And come back to it whenever you'd like.

A Little Meditation
BASIC MINDFULNESS

Let's start with a five-minute exercise. Five minutes is just enough time to let the mind drop into the body. And letting the mind drop into the body is a great way to release some of the spinning, storming thoughts that make us unhappy for no great reason. So let's start by getting comfy. When we're meditating, it's nice to be relaxed and at ease, but it's also helpful to be energized and alert in your body. You can try sitting on a cushion on the floor, or in a chair, or on your couch. Your posture can vary—the point is just to make sure your body feels supported but also awake. Close your eyes if you like, or keep a soft, downward gaze.

Now, take a few deep breaths. As you exhale, let go of any thoughts or worries or plans you might have running through your head.

Allow your breath to return to a natural rhythm, and simply feel your body from the inside out. Explore your inner weather patterns. Is it sunny inside? Or stormy? Or maybe you can't feel anything at all. That's okay. Just stay curious about this experience of having a body. Do you feel tension or ease in different parts of your body? Do you feel warm or cool? Do you feel pressure where you're sitting? Use your awareness to feel all your bodily sensations as they come and go.

Of course, your mind will wander and get lost in thoughts as you do this. This is normal and natural and supposed to happen. When you notice that you're distracted, that's okay. You haven't failed at meditation. This recognition of your wandering mind is actually a moment of *sati*, of remembering to be aware. Just come back to feeling your body in the present moment.

Mindfulness is simply setting the intention to be present and then training your mind to come back again and again. In this meditation, we're focusing on body sensations. So keep coming back to your body and feel it from the inside. Let's do this for a few more breaths.

Congrats! You just meditated! You were cultivating mindfulness, or present moment awareness. You can also do this mental practice throughout your day. Whenever you remember, come back to your body and feel its sensations, posture, temperature. As you continue to read, you can train in this way, remembering to feel your body every now and again. It's as simple as that.

#FACTS

When I started my own meditation practice, back in 2001, there was practically no decent meditation research on the impacts of meditation on the brain, emotions, behavior. In fact, for my senior college thesis, I told my advisor I wanted to write a paper on the impacts of meditation on kids with ADHD. She looked at me pityingly and said, "That's very nice. But what on earth does it have to do with psychology?"

I wrote the paper anyway. And the very next year Richard J. Davidson, the renowned neuroscientist and public intellectual, started publishing really good, hard-hitting, hard-science research on meditation. He triggered an avalanche. These days, over seven thousand studies have been published. So many it's hard to even sift through the findings. So I'll break it down for you. Really simple. Here are the top three reasons to meditate:

1. It lowers stress.
2. It helps you focus.
3. And it might make you a better human.

Meditation Lowers Stress

If there's one thing meditation definitely, definitely, definitely, for-sure-according-to-science does, it's lower stress. There are a ton of studies that show this. Good studies. Really good studies. Studies with active control groups, and biomarkers, and robust samples, oh my! I won't get into every one of these studies right this moment, but here's one to give you just a taste.

In this particularly fun experiment, some scientists at Stanford University took a bunch of folks with social anxiety disorder and asked them to write down their worst anxiety experiences.[2] Sound awful? Keep reading. They wrote about things like being trapped in a subway car while having a panic attack. Or being forced to give a speech in front of derisive classmates.

Then the researchers running the experiment put these same subjects in an fMRI machine, which is like being wrapped in a whirring, clacking, sewer pipe, and they read back to them the very stories they had just written, along with their most damning self-assessments, such as, "I am incompetent."

Unsurprisingly, the circuits of their brains related to stress and anxiety lit up like a Christmas tree.

The experimenters then split the group in two. They taught one group mindfulness techniques and they taught the other group to do arithmetic to distract from negative thinking. And then they ran all the subjects through the fMRI machine all over again, complete with listening to their anxiety journals and painful self-assessments.

Any guesses about what happened? Spoiler: The arithmetic group didn't improve. They were still super stressed by the experience. But the group that learned mindfulness? They saw dips in their brains' stress response—they were less freaked out than they'd been before.

Other studies have compared mindfulness to cognitive reappraisal, mindfulness to relaxation, and mindfulness to just being put on a waitlist. And in each case, mindfulness lowered stress significantly more than the competing treatment.

So we can say with real confidence that mindfulness lowers stress levels. But how? Good question. Let's take a look. Mindfulness, as we just mentioned, is the simple act of being aware. Nonjudgmentally and on purpose.

Simple enough, right?

But the crazy thing is that being aware, nonjudgmentally and on purpose, breaks the cycle of rumination. And rumination, it turns out, is a hellacious contemporary affliction, a gruesome epidemic of the soul, the psychological cholera of hyper-tech, post-industrialist societies.

To understand this, it's helpful to get a handle on how our stress response works.

Humans evolved in dangerous environments. Every once in a while something super bad happened, and our bodies needed to respond. Our heart rates would go through the roof, our blood would be pulled out of our extremities, and our nervous systems would go berserk. That way we could run like hell or fight like hell or just freeze and play dead. Way back then, though, it was pretty obvious when the danger had passed. And when it passed the body would calm down, the mind would chill out, and we'd go back to happily picking berries and gossiping about who we wanted to have babies with. Back then, there wasn't a lot of room for rumination. There was danger, it passed, we moved on.

These days, though, your nervous system responds to a hostile email or a politically charged news report or a coworker saying something jacked in much the same way your ancestors used to respond to a saber-toothed tiger. Only now, email and news stories are way more prevalent than saber-toothed tigers ever were. So the body ends up in a continual state of activation, making your emotions and thoughts just spin and spin and spin.

And spinning thoughts are super bad for you. They super freak you out. And they lead to a host of stress-related bad stuff like depression, anxiety, and any number of chronic physical ailments.

When you practice the simple act of bringing attention back to your left foot, or your breath, or even nonjudgmentally bringing awareness to your thoughts, the spinning mind slows its roll and you're more able to relate to your experience in a calm, collected, and warmhearted way. Stress levels go down. A kind of friendliness develops. And all this is a very good thing.

AND ANOTHER THING...
Letting Go of Expectations

To be honest, I sometimes worry a little when I tell people about the research on mindfulness and meditation. I mean, it's exciting stuff. I love talking about it. I love getting people excited about this thing I've been excited about my entire adult life.

But I want to be careful, too. First, because the science is complicated, there's more research to be done, and I'm simplifying to make a point or two here. But most importantly, telling everybody how helpful meditation is might actually short-circuit the very ways that meditation is helpful.

Let me explain.

Meditation practice is primarily about letting go of expectations. It's about being present with whatever's here, no matter what is here. That includes pleasant physical sensations and unpleasant physical sensations. It includes nice emotional feelings, and not-so-nice emotional feelings. It also includes every conceivable kind of thought.

The power of meditation is not that all these things cease and desist. It's not that we stop thoughts in meditation—we don't stop thoughts in meditation. It's not that our unpleasant emotions and painful bodily experiences disappear. It's simply that we get really good at letting our experience be exactly as it is, moment by moment, no matter what it is, with warmth and friendliness and maybe even some steady sense of presence. And this engaged acceptance in itself is transformative.

So as you read all the scientific stuff, I hope you'll be inspired. I hope you'll sit down in a chair or on a cushion and try meditation for yourself.

But just remember: Once you've been inspired to sit down and give it a try, don't look for some special experience. Don't block out your thoughts or your feelings. Don't think this meditation practice will make you into some kind of superhuman with

> no perceivable problems. Just keep coming back to
> what is, again and again. That's the skill we're really
> looking to develop.

Meditation Also Helps You Focus

At first blush, increased focus probably doesn't sound like such a big deal. But think about it. Pretty much every worthwhile thing you do—from playing an instrument to cooking a meal to writing code—requires some level of baseline attentiveness. And the more attentive you are, the better things go.

Take, for example, your daily workflow. You get to your desk. Check your email. Check your voicemail. Check your Slack channel. Check your to-do list. Three people stop by asking for stuff. You get a text from your mom. You get a news alert on your phone. And then somehow you have to find a way to sift through the noise and get cracking.

This is where a lot of people get stuck. There's so much information. Like a flood of beeping, buzzing, binging noise, and each piece of information is waving flags and flashing lights telling you it's really, really, really important. So how do you actually choose what to focus on first? And then next? And on and on, moment to moment, throughout your day?

Well, mindfulness training—just that simple act of being intentionally aware again and again—can help. But don't take my word for it. Let's take a look at some of the research:[3]

- People who take an eight-week mindfulness-based stress reduction course see a big jump in focus.[4]
- Long-term meditators show far better focus than well-matched controls.[5]
- People who do a three-month retreat see a big bump in focus, and it stays with them long after the retreat ends.[6]
- Ten minutes of mindfulness heals the break in focus associated with multitasking.[7]
- Eight minutes of mindfulness decreases mind-wandering.[8]
- Ten hours of mindfulness training increases baseline levels of both focus and working memory.[9]

So mindfulness works a kind of focus magic. Coming back to the breath again and again trains you to bring your attention to just about anything. If you can pay attention to your breath, you can pay attention to your work. You can pay attention to your pickleball game. You can pay attention in bed. In other words, your sustained awareness in all these areas will likely get a good little bump. And the more you practice, the bigger the bump you'll see.

But all this can seem a little vague and brainy. So let me tell you a story about a meditator I know pretty well who saw big gains from learning focus. His name is Craig, and he's my husband and the coauthor of this book. Craig got into meditation when he was pretty young. And it's a good thing, too, because he was kind of a mess.

Craig and I had really different experiences in high school. While I was getting straight As and playing volleyball, he was getting high and playing rock music and always on the edge of being thrown out of somebody's history class for mouthing off about left-wing politics. Without getting into the details, Craig seemed an unlikely candidate for sitting still and feeling his breath. Then, when he was fifteen, he picked up a book by Joseph Goldstein. And he had one of those moments. Things in his mind kind of just came together. "Yes," he thought, "this is my jam."

This was 1994. There were no meditation apps. No one he knew was talking about mindfulness. Meditation, in fact, was still something relegated to people who wore flowing dresses and cymbals on their fingers and talked about astral planes. Or else Buddhist monks in orange robes in Asia. Or at least that's what people in his secular, middle-class, workaday world mostly thought.

Still, Joseph's book in hand, Craig started to meditate. Cross-legged on his bedroom floor in the suburbs of New York City. And like most of us, the first thing he noticed was that his mind was a blizzard of thoughts, desires, resentments, distractions. He literally could not bring awareness to his breath for more than a few seconds.

He tried. Then he tried again. And again. And again. But he could not get a handle on it. His mind was like a rodeo bull. He just got thrown and thrown.

After days, he saw no improvement. Weeks of floor-sitting brought nothing. In fact, if anything, he felt crazier, sitting there, alone on the floor of his room, trying to muscle his attention into place.

Finally, he decided he needed a teacher. There was no way he was going to wrangle his own mind without guidance. And so, long story short, and after several false starts, he found himself driving his father's car to the dairy country of upstate New York on a freezing November day a week before his seventeenth birthday, on his way to his first weekend retreat.

Things lined up after that. He went home and talked to his new meditation teacher every week on the phone. He started sitting ten minutes a day, then twenty, then thirty. But things still didn't change overnight. In fact, college wasn't so great for Craig at first. He was plagued by self-doubt, procrastination, anxiety, and the very real inability to actually sit down and get stuff done. He managed to do well enough in most of his classes. But he was frustrated. He really liked what he was studying and wanted to knock college out of the park.

Over the summer, after his first year, he signed up for a monthlong retreat at that same center in upstate New York. Halfway through the retreat, something became clear: he wanted to take a semester off from college and sit a really long meditation retreat. And, because he's kind of an extremist, that's exactly what he did. Yes, when Craig was nineteen years old, he ended up sitting a five-month meditation retreat.

When he came back to college after that, things felt different. Almost overnight, he was doing really well. Where before he had trouble wrangling his attention and getting things done, now he could sit for four-hour stretches at the library, poring over Kant's indecipherable syllogisms, without getting antsy. He went from being a kid who used to get thrown out of class in high school to being a kid who won awards in college.

What happened? In a word, he learned to focus. Hour after hour on retreat, he brought his attention back to his breath. Again and again. Until he could place his attention on something and it would mostly just stay there. I'm not saying Craig is some perfect human. I live with him, so I know that just this week he left his keys in the ignition of our car at the mall, forgot his phone on an airplane, and got overwhelmed with deadlines for this very book. But I can say he's mostly pretty focused a lot of the time. And that makes him a really decent life partner, a good friend, and somebody who, generally speaking, gets stuff done.

So it's not just in the research. Focus can change your days. Because you need focus to make things happen. You need focus to listen to the people you love, earn money, and keep yourself on track in the midst of the deafening storm of information you wade through every hour.

Mindfulness, the simple act of training attention, leads to just that kind of focus. The question then becomes, What will you do with that focus?

Meditation Might Make You a Better Human

A few years ago a super-cool scientist named Helen Weng did a study at the University of Wisconsin–Madison, where she was then a graduate student. It was published in one of the best psych journals around, and the results blew everybody away.[10]

Helen wanted to study compassion. In particular, she wanted to know if meditation training could, perhaps, increase compassionate action.

To find out, she took some undergrads and divided them into two groups. The groups were just about identical in age and gender, and at the beginning of the study they tested fairly evenly on baseline compassion rates. She then sent the two groups through two different trainings. The first group went through a two-week meditation training focused on compassion. The second group went through a two-week cognitive reappraisal training that was designed to increase positive thoughts.

To measure progress, Helen gave everybody an fMRI scan before and after the trainings. At the end, she also had everybody play a game that was designed to test altruism. For the game, she gave everybody twenty bucks. Then, during the game, participants in the study watched a "dictator" steal money from a "victim." Of course, the dictator and victim weren't real players, but the study subjects didn't know that. They just knew that they had this twenty bucks that they'd been given. And they knew they could give some of that money to the victim. And if they gave some of their money to the victim, the rules of the game would force the dictator to reimburse the victim. In other words, they could give some of their very own money, money they'd earned from being in this arduous study, to right the wrong.

Curious what Helen found?

First off, she found that those who underwent the meditation training showed greater activation in the brain circuits usually associated with empathy, emotion regulation, and positive affect. So that's already interesting.

But here's the real kicker: the folks who did two weeks of compassion meditation gave nearly *twice* as much money as the other group.

So meditation training not only impacted the way people *felt* about the victim (that's the brain part), it also changed the way they *acted* toward the victim. They were literally more willing to make a sacrifice to improve another person's situation. Pretty cool, right?

So maybe meditation can make us better humans—more compassionate, more ready to respond to others. And in fact, there's other research on this now, too. One study I like a lot, which came out of Yale a few years ago, showed that teaching white people kindness meditation reduces their bias toward racial minorities.[11] Other studies have shown that meditation increases social connectedness,[12] that it boosts compassionate responses to suffering,[13] that it can reduce prejudice toward homeless people,[14] that it combats ageism,[15] and on and on. This compassion effect is a big deal.

Our culture is multicultural, multi-everything, has always been, and is getting more so every day. It's pretty obvious that we're going to have to find a way to all live together. The evidence suggests that meditation can help with that.

AND ANOTHER THING...

Mindfulness Can Dismantle White Supremacy

As I've already stated, I'm white. Like just about every white person I know, I used to think I didn't have a problem with race. I was taught to be "color blind." I was taught we're all equal, we're all good, and we shouldn't see the differences.

The problem is, this kind of thinking paints over the very real differences between what white people experience versus just about everybody else in the United States—not to mention around the world. We're talking about serious disparities in health, in education, and in access to the most basic resources.

This massive imbalance reflects the reality of white supremacy. Even though we usually associate white supremacy with hate speech and hate crimes, that's actually just the tail end of a big curve, where the entire curve represents all the ways white people get a little leg up in just about every moment of their lives, while people of color get a little nudge down in so many moments of their lives. And if we're going to stand up in the middle of the storm, it's not only about less stress and more focus; it's also about what's worth standing up for. Meditation (plus wisdom and goodness and clarity) can help us figure this out.

I wasn't confronted with my unwitting participation in white supremacy until I was in my late twenties. Like I said, I grew up in a liberal white town, surrounded by liberal white people. Pretty much all of my friends were white. I had a couple POC (people of color) friends, but we definitely didn't have the tough conversations about whiteness.

Then, in 2010, I joined a two-year teacher-training program through Spirit Rock. We were all learning to be community leaders and meditation teachers. But the really cool (and really challenging) thing was that the group taking part in the training was very diverse. Out of the one hundred or so folks I trained with, about half were POC. A whole slew were queer-identified. We were from all over the country and all walks of life.

Things were not always smooth. Our teachers, Larry Yang and Gina Sharpe, talked a lot about "breaking together" rather than "breaking apart." And break we did. There were arguments, walkouts, spirited councils, and feelings of every kind got expressed—sometimes loudly.

Through it all, though, we meditated. Sometimes in a big, sprawling circle. Sometimes scattered around the hall. We meditated outside and inside. Alone and together. In small groups, in big groups. When things were sweet and placid, we meditated. When things were choppy and raw, we meditated.

I don't know how we would all have gotten through it together if not for meditation. Mindfulness was, I think, our ballast. Every time the ship started to roll, meditation brought us back upright in the storm. Together we'd find a way to take a few breaths, and keep talking, then take a few breaths, and keep listening. And, gradually, breath by breath, moment by heart-rending moment, we started to find each other.

So there are approximately one bajillion reasons why you should meditate. The top three reasons, as I've just mentioned, are that you'll be less stressed, more focused, and you might even stumble your way into slightly better humanhood. Meditation will, in other words, make you *somewhat* less of a hot mess.

But meditation, this thing you do with your mind, is just one part of the sloppy collage we're throwing together in these six sprawling chapters. In fact, the meat of what we have to say is still to come. Because while mindfulness is the foundation for a really pretty decent life, you'll need more than a foundation to survive the onslaught. You'll have to use the calm and focus and clarity you develop through meditation like a spotlight—a spotlight that we'll now help you turn toward how you speak, what you do, and who you are at work and at school and at home.

Sound good? Great. Let's start with not being a jerk.

DON'T BE A JERK

Craig

In this chapter, I'm going to try to convince you not to be a jerk. I mean, you're probably already not a jerk. I'm sure you're usually basically a very nice human. But if you're anything like me, you're a usually nice human who flips out sometimes, says things he doesn't mean, or maybe even says things he *does* mean and then encounters the rippling layers of consequences of those things down the line. Therefore, my goal here is to persuade you to do less of the jerk-like stuff you might be doing in your everyday life, and more of the pro-social, happy-making stuff you're probably *also* already doing.

But I'm getting ahead of myself. Let's kick this party off with a brief contemplation.

Please take a minute and think of a real jerk. This could be a stupid terrible jerk from your present life. It could be an awful disgusting jerk from your past. Or maybe even a historical jerk or a big-time political jerk. Whoever this jerk is, just make sure they really embody jerkiness for you.

Got your jerk? Good.

Now, I'd like you to start to catalog this person's badness. In other words, what makes them such a jerk? Please think of all the qualities that make this individual particularly unbearable. What makes them terrible? What is it about your special jerk that makes you want to ring their neck or flee the building?

Have you let your imagination run wild? Got a good little list going?

Okay. Now you can gently snap out of your reverie and look around the room. Orient yourself. Shake off the dirty. I know it's never fun to think about the Skeletors.

So let's look together at that compendium of jerkdom you just assembled. What exactly was on that list of unforgivable attributes this particular jerk personifies?

My guess is there are all kinds of things. This person talks behind your back. Or they threw sand in your eyes when you were ten. Or they're racist. Or just plain damned ignorant. Or a horrible bore who won't let you get a word in at parties. Or they've done something truly terrible to you or someone you love.

But small or big, if you look closely, I think you'll find that all jerks have one thing unswervingly in common. A jerk, put simply, is someone who causes harm.

BEING A JERK IS A REAL DOWNER

So jerks cause harm. They hurt others, in small and big ways. They cut you off in traffic or talk on the phone really loud in coffee shops or threaten the democratic norms you've always believed were intrinsic to the functioning of a civilized society. That's why we don't like jerks. Because they're looking out for number one and triggering avalanches of chaos everywhere they set their feet to walking.

But are jerks happy themselves? Well, an expeditious jaunt through the history books tells us, undeniably, no. Jerks are the most miserable, paranoid, and all-around apprehensive sad sacks around. They might start out all right, sure. The early days of a Stalin or a Pol Pot are often suffused with purpose. But as they let the jerkiness overtake them, as they lock up their enemies and stomp out their critics on the way to whatever grand plan they've imagined for themselves and their nation, slowly but surely they end up isolated and anemic, essentially friendless, a power to be managed rather than loved.

And that's the great jerks. Little jerks usually don't even get that far.

Let's have a look at some research to drive this point home. Unfortunately, psychologists don't really go around calling people jerks (not in public anyway). Instead, they talk about things like *pathological narcissism* and a bunch of other fancy-pants names that essentially add up to someone acting like a no-good, insufferable pissant. Nevertheless, the research suggests that jerks don't have a very fun time.

Take narcissists, for example. A narcissist is one special kind of jerky jerk. You know the type. She's that blowhard in the office or at the gym or in your bowling club who really,

really needs you to think she's so very awesome. By definition, narcissists' goals are all about them, they have a really tough time being part of a team, and they tend to take any statement that is not direct praise as an interpersonal affront.

Does that sound like a fun way to live? Definitely not.

In fact, psychologists have now established that narcissists—that is, people who are exploitative of others, self-centered, and quick to talk up their own game—have a terrible time with stress, struggle with commonplace setbacks, and can barely handle the ups and downs of everyday life. For instance, a study[1] at the University of Michigan put undergrads through a stressful situation in the lab. They found that the more narcissistic the participants were, the higher their stress response. Another study[2] found that, when confronted with everyday frustrations, narcissists produced more stress hormones than their less self-aggrandizing counterparts. Other studies have found that narcissists are quick to anger,[3] surprisingly impulsive, and that they tend to engage in self-defeating behaviors for no obvious reason.[4] And that's just the tip of the iceberg when we're talking about all the ways narcissists sabotage their own joy.

So a jerk is somebody who causes harm. In big ways and small ways. They're selfish, maybe even narcissistic, and being that way actually doesn't lead to contentment or good cheer. It leads to misery and isolation. Therefore—and I hope you're coming to this conclusion now in your own mind and heart—it would be wonderful not to be a jerk.

But here's the kicker, a time-honored semi-Buddhist insight: all of us have a little jerk living inside us somewhere. The part of us that wants what it wants, that doesn't care about others' feelings, that's totally going to snag that parking spot outside the grocery store even though the mom with two kids so obviously got there first. And if we want to be happy long term, with flourishing friendships and a more-or-less stable sense of purpose and good cheer, we'll need to stay alert to that self-sabotaging part of ourselves and choose something different.

So in the end, what we want to do is practice some version of mindfulness. We want to see clearly the jerkiness in others, and navigate those relationships. Conversely, we want to see the jerkiness in ourselves, and mitigate the moments when these tendencies flare up. Along the way you'll want to keep an eye on your mind, keep an eye on your heart, and notice what you're doing. It's good to spot when you're living up to your basic values, and important to know when you're not.

On that note, let's talk about some basic values I bet we probably share. We'll start with the really-truly-basic and then go from there. For example: don't kill.

DON'T KILL

I'll just go ahead and assume you didn't kill anybody today. Congratulations! You've just accomplished the first, most fundamental level of not being a jerk.

Now, you might think "no killing" is a low bar to set. But it's worth noting that, for the vast run of human history, most cultures condoned killing under a host of circumstances that we would find a little surprising today. Like blood feuds, petty theft, adultery, witchcraft, really mean insults, or just when the other guy was from a different tribe or culture and you kind of wanted his stuff. And of course anybody who picks up the occasional newspaper knows humanity has yet to master the art of nonviolence.

So not killing each other is a big deal. And we should all be good and proud of that. But, as with all these pieces of advice, there are layers.

In today's world, there are lots of ways that we commit acts of violence besides using a bayonet. Even if we're not actually poisoning our neighbors to get our hands on their HDTV, we're still, most of us, participating in acts that harm—and most of these are verbal, in one way or another. Perhaps a story could help illustrate this point.

I lived in a Zen monastery for a while. Six years, all told. Now, when I tell people I lived in a Zen monastery in the remote mountains of Colorado—when I show them pictures of the Japanese tea house and the black meditation cushions all in a row—they usually say something like "That must have been so peaceful."

Yeah, no. It wasn't. A monastery is a training ground. You're up at 3:30 in the morning. You're meditating for hours every day. There's no personal space. You don't get days off. And all of you are stuck together in your black robes and your weird habits for months at a time—no one coming, no one going, and no way out. It's like a pot you put on to boil and then forgot about. Or like a submarine that's just dived way down and won't see sunlight for a season.

Add to that the fact that I lived my time in the monastery for the better part of my twenties—a time when I had yet to become the ultra-smooth communicator that I am today (my closest friends will recognize this as sarcasm)—and you get a recipe for some exhilarating conflagrations.

Enter Anthony. Anthony owned a bookstore in the Mission in San Francisco. He was a longtime Zen student, in his fifties, with a crew cut, a bag full of government conspiracy theories, and an excessively short fuse.

When Anthony came to the monastery, he had the misfortune of being under my auspices. I was the work leader—a position that entailed me, at twenty-five, telling everyone else (age range eighteen to eighty) what to do. Not that I was particularly dictatorial, I think. But busy, for sure. And a little visionary sometimes. There was stuff to get done and I had a plan and I wanted people—e.g., Anthony—to step to the vision.

And so I ran my meetings like clockwork. Or as my friend Matt later told me, like boot camp. Okay, I admit it, there were spreadsheets. There were timelines. And there was building frustration on my part, since the actual world was, very often, not conforming to my spreadsheets and my timelines.

It all came to a head on a crystalline February day. Thirty strapping volunteers from a local college were on their way to campus. We were going to do fire mitigation—a pressing concern for the monastery, since our surrounding desert mountains were a tinderbox of brush and low branches, just waiting to go up in flames.

I'd arranged for three professionals to arrive with their chain saws. They'd be cutting all day. I'd arranged for each available member of the monastic community to lead a work group of five college kids. They'd be hauling all day. I was in the middle of downloading the vision, psyching up the troops, clarifying the details, when Anthony raised his hand.

"Yes, Anthony," I said.

"What time is lunch?" he said.

I was flummoxed. Lunch? We were about to move mountains! "Who cares?" I said.

And then I went back to explicating the hauling routes and assigning the responsibilities.

After the meeting, I was walking into the kitchen when Anthony came from behind, spun me around by the shoulder, and threw me up against the wall.

Suddenly, everything went very slowly. I noticed that his face was a startling shade of red, almost purple. His eyes looked red, too. There was a single bead of sweat on his forehead. And his breath smelled like coffee and milk.

As Anthony shook me and slammed me, he was saying things. For example, "If you ever talk to me that way again, I will cut your throat."

But already my mind was tracking back over the last several minutes. Clearly, I had done something that really pissed Anthony off. At first I was a little too dumb to know what it was. But my mind tracked back, tracked back, and then realized it was that moment I'd blown off his question about lunch.

Simultaneously, I saw there existed a whole range of options before me, almost like radio stations. Except instead of choosing between NPR and classic rock, my mind started flipping through disparate cultural scripts, little memes that might be appropriate for just such an occasion. For instance, I'm from New York, and the New York radio station was enticing me to throw a punch. Thankfully, though, the Buddhist radio station also clicked on, even stronger. I saw, all of a sudden, how I had come into the meeting all jazzed up, a little manic. I saw how my empathy in the meeting was low. I saw how I had needlessly insulted Anthony, made him feel small. And I saw my low empathy and subsequent belittling as the cause of the present death threat.

So I relaxed. "Anthony," I said. "I messed up. Sorry. Just one of those days."

He looked confused for a moment. Then I watched his face cycle through its own range of emotions—watched him try to remain angry, then confused again, then sad, then just tired. He dropped my shirt and walked away.

I wish I could say I always have that level of insight. It would have been nice, for example, to hold my tongue that time in the trailer in the New Mexico wilderness, when a benzo-popping Forest Service employee named Jane threw a blender full of hot soup at my head. (Yes, that really happened.) In that moment with Jane, I had a similar radio station moment, in which I watched a bunch of options whiz right by me—and chose, consciously, unequivocally—to go to war. We ended up screaming at each other for forty-five minutes. And the next day, the director of our Forest Service division fired us both.

That time I was twenty-two. So one tidy story is that between the ages of twenty-two, when I went to war unnecessarily with Jane, and twenty-eight, when I kept the peace, more or less, with Anthony, I had made great spiritual progress. Still a jerk, kind of. But I knew I was a jerk and acted with benevolence about my jerkiness.

The truth, though, is that spiritual progress is a bumpy road. Not so much an ever-upward line of transcendent growth. More like a series of peaks and valleys. In which you fall flat on your face in the valley. In a swamp. With mosquitoes. And no bug spray. Then dust yourself off and keep working at it.

BE A BLOCK OF WOOD

So what should we do when we want to take somebody's head off? Well, step one, as mentioned above, is don't literally take their head off. There are laws against that. Step two is what the Dalai Lama calls "the ethic of restraint."[5] In other words, you take a breath. You don't fire off that email. You don't spit out the brilliant zinger. You don't kill—not even with words. Instead, you talk to a friend—and you choose a cool-headed friend who'll give you good advice. Or you go for a walk. And then you don't say or do a damn thing until you're ready to say something . . . if not productive, then at least not destructive.

As Shantideva, the great sixth-century Buddhist pundit, put it, until you get back your composure, "remain like a block of wood."

Sounds easy enough, right? It's not easy. Not at all. First, because you'll have to sit with a tremendous swirling discomfort. And second, because *sometimes stuff needs to get said.*

Let's start with discomfort. This is where mindfulness comes in. Let's say, just as an example, that you're a cis-hetero guy like me and you're married to a cis-hetero woman (you know, like Devon). And you really like each other. It's a good relationship. But there are things that your wonderful life partner does that make you a little bonkers. Who cares what. Let's say it's the way she drives. She's a speed freak, and you grew up with your grandmother and think everyone should drive 53 miles per hour on the highway. Now you're in the car with her, and she's driving. She's weaving her way between tractor trailers, gracefully threading traffic like a skier in the Super-G finals at the Winter Olympics. Your blood starts to boil. She's doing all the wrong things. You're not scared, mind you. Just annoyed.

This would be a moment, perhaps, to remain like a block of wood. To shut your mouth, take a breath, and get a little internal. If you can do this without your partner even knowing, that's ninja territory. Otherwise, you might want to let them know you're going to take a minute. This sounds cheesy and artificial—and it is—but once your loved ones start to associate this weirdly mindful behavior with fewer temper tantrums from your side, they'll often get on board in a big way.

BUILD KINDNESS

So to recap: restraint is good when you're flipping out and it would be better to hold your tongue. But not everything is restraint. You can't walk around all day like a block of wood. That's just for those moments when you're about to fire off a shot at your boss who just fired off a shot at you— knowing full well you're about to lose your job. Those are the moments when it's cool to be a little woody.

But what about those times when you can't just remain like a block of wood? Times when things just *need to get said*. For example, a while back I wrote a blog post that made some ill-informed generalizations about the differences between Asian and Western Buddhist teachers. I got the following email from Dr. Bonnie Duran, who is a professor of social work and public health at the University of Washington, an indigenous scholar, and a kickass meditation teacher:

Hello Craig,

Hope you are both well and happy.

Just read your post. Wow—Really? Why?

As I read your essay, I hear strong echoes of a Eurocentric, patriarchal, commodified "view." The huge sweeping racial generalizations and comparisons of your essay are major tools of a settler colonial system that is still alive and well in the US. I'm sure you didn't mean to cause harm, but harm there is. Plenty of reading on decolonizing in the drop boxes below.

Wishing us all much peace and ease, (big hug to Devon)
Bonnie

So should Dr. Duran have "remained like a block of wood?" Should she have held her tongue and kept the peace? Of course not. What I wrote actually *was* Eurocentric, patriarchal, and commodified, and she was kind enough to point it out. She didn't mince words in her email to me. She said exactly what she saw. But what I notice when I read back on this exchange is how unfailingly kind she is. Clarity and kindness, together. That combination is powerful. And Dr. Duran, with her years of meditation training, has managed to build a heart of kindness and then extend that to others.

So there are times when *not* speaking up is an act of harm. And in order to engage with others in a respectful and productive way, we want to cultivate a sense of warmth and fluidity. Preemptive kindness. An axiological stance of friendliness toward the world. But how? Back to meditation. Meditation is about more than just calming the mind. It's also about cultivating an atmosphere of warmth and positive regard—for yourself, for others. It's about finding a way to live in the world that corroborates your deepest aspirations. Sound good? So let's try some.

A Little Meditation
KINDNESS

You can do this meditation in five minutes, if you'd like. I first started doing these kindness meditations years ago when I was living in the monastery. At first it was hard for me to get a feel for them, but as I kept inclining the mind toward kindness, I noticed parts of myself softening, the voice in my head easing up. I definitely recommend this meditation to anybody who could use a little more kindness in their life. And that's pretty much all of us.

As always, let's start by finding a comfortable posture, either sitting or lying down. Obviously if you're reading this book, it'll be hard to close your eyes. So you can keep them open. Or read a few sentences and then close your eyes. Then read a few more. Up to you. Whatever you do, you'll want to just relax. Don't worry too much about whether you're doing it right. Don't worry too much about being a great meditator. In fact, just don't worry too much.

Now let's bring a warm awareness to your body. Just feel your body. With a sense of friendliness, a sort of grassroots kindness. Feel your hands. Feel your feet.

Then bring that warm awareness to the area of your heart. Notice any sensations in the heart area—throbbing, humming, tingling, numb, whatever. Also, start to notice any emotions that might be here, in the heart. Just kind of take the temperature. Get a sense of things.

One important point: You don't need to get rid of any-thing, don't need to feel differently or better. If you're numb, you're numb. No problem. If you're sad, that's how it is. Angry? That's okay, too.

And often we're a whole bunch of things all at once. Which is also not a problem.

Now from this sense of the heart—of just being with your heart—let's call up an image of a good friend. Some-one you like. Someone that's easy for you. They've got your back. Sure, they tick you off every once in a while. But es-sentially it's a good relationship—all in all, you want them to be happy, and you want to contribute to that.

Got an image? Great.

Now let's lean a little into this sense that your friend wants to be happy. Just like you, just like everybody, he or she or they really want to be happy. They want to be safe. They want to be healthy. They'd like some peace. See if you can get a sense of that for them.

And now let's just begin to wish them well, using some traditional phrases.

May you be safe.
May you be happy.
May you be healthy.
May you be peaceful and at ease.

Just continue thinking about your friend, repeating these phrases silently to yourself. And maybe after some time, you can imagine your friend filling up with happiness. Imagine your friend getting lighter. Imagine your friend getting happier. Imagine them smiling. Filled with joy.

Nice job. You've completed a kindness meditation. It's great to start with a friend when you do this at first, somebody who's pretty easy for you. Once you get the hang of that, though, it can be really helpful to bring this same kindness, this wishing well, to yourself. *May I be safe, may I be happy*, etc. Then you can extend that general caring out to people you don't know so well, and even to people you don't like so much, and then to everyone, everywhere, without exception.

THE BENEFITS OF KINDNESS MEDITATION

Now that you've done some, I'll throw in a little pitch for kindness meditation. Because there's actually quite a bit of research on it. And what we know is that, when practiced with a qualified instructor over a period of six or eight weeks, this type of meditation can lead to an increased sense of social connection,[6] improvements in overall mood, increased sense of purpose in life, reductions in depression,[7] and even, as mentioned in the previous chapter, decreases in implicit bias. So kindness meditation is a powerful practice, and one that can really change your experience of others. Here's a quick story on that count.

I've finished my PhD now, thank god. But it was a long, difficult process, filled, at least for me, with unexpected turbulence, twists and turns, interpersonal difficulties, departmental dramas, and all the rest.

Things kind of peaked in the third year of my program in counseling psychology at the University of Wisconsin–Madison. Early on in the program I'd made some dumb mistakes, had kind of kicked the hornet's nest of the bureaucracy, and things had begun to spin out before I got my head on straight and learned the ropes. So there was damage, and mostly in my feeling about the program. Unlike my master's program, where I'd felt incredibly supported and welcomed, I didn't feel I fit in too sweetly with the swing of things in my PhD program.

Right around my low point—year three, spring—my department hosted a brilliant, famous psychotherapist for a daylong workshop. When I walked in, it was the same old feeling—anxiety, out-of-placeness, a sense that people were kind of looking at me funny. Call it paranoia. Or a bad case of the jitters. It was unpleasant. I sat with that for the first few hours of the workshop. Then we broke for lunch and I rode my bike across campus to teach kindness meditation at the School of Veterinary Medicine. I taught a class to students first, then a class to faculty, then I rode my bike back to the workshop.

When I walked in, lunch was just ending. People were milling about, getting ready to take their seats. First one person said hi to me. Then another person said hi to me. It seemed that everyone in the room was smiling—and half of them appeared to be smiling, kind of beatifically, at *me*.

Wow, I thought to myself initially, they must have had a great lunch. But no. They'd had the same Qdoba spread the department always serves.

And then it struck me. Nothing had changed. Except me. I had just spent a couple hours teaching kindness to vets. And it had rubbed off. I was seeing the world through kindness-tinted lenses. And it was beautiful.

AND ANOTHER THING...

You'll Need a Posse

Stories like this sound great, don't they? I was having a bad time, then I tinkered with my mind-set, then I had a good time. A + B = C, right?

But it's actually not that simple. It's not that I just went and did a little kindness meditation and then everything was hunky-dory. Truth be told, that was just a single lucid moment—a beautiful moment, a moment of clarifying insight that I now use as a touchstone when I'm feeling blue. But just a moment. It didn't heal all my problems or set me straight for all time.

In fact, if I'm going to be 100 percent honest with you, these kinds of clarifying insights are few and far between. A lot of the time most of us are just sloshing around in the dregs of our bad mental habits.

Which is why it's so very important to have friends on the path. Because if we're all alone on this little journey of mindfulness and good living, we tend to get pretty lost. Not only will we get caught up in the aforementioned bad mental habits, but we'll get hypnotized by all the noxious ideologies of our dysregulated cultural moment (see chapter 5 for more on these ideologies).

So if you're starting to jibe with what we're saying here—if you think you'd like to meditate and not be a jerk and maybe give a little and all the rest—the first thing to do, in our opinion, is find other people who jibe with this kind of stuff, too. In person, if you can. That would be best. But if you live in a place where nobody's talking about this stuff, you can always find a home online.

You'll be really glad you did.

Okay, we were just talking about kindness. Let's get back to that.

BE HELPFUL

You know the other great thing about cultivating kindness, though? It triggers our natural love of altruism. Now, you may object: *A natural love of altruism?* You might say, *Hogwash. I watch the evening news. I know what people are up to. And it has nothing to do with looking out for your fellow mortals.* But here's the thing: humans, by nature, love to be helpful. We do. Don't let the cynicism of our post-factual era get you down. The truth is that we're built to aid each other. For example, Michael Tomasello, a developmental psychologist at Duke University, has run a long series of experiments measuring helping behaviors in young children. From the age of about eighteen months, kids start to help—they help each other, and they help adults.[8]

In one experiment,[9] a researcher is hanging clothes. She drops a clothespin. Kids in the study run over, without being asked, to pick up the clothespin and give it to the woman who dropped it. In another, a researcher is carrying a bunch of books and can't get a cupboard open. Kids in the study run over to open the cupboard. Unasked.

Put on these glasses and look around for an hour. Walk down a city street and watch people help each other. Watch as a guy holds the door for a teenager carrying groceries. Watch as a stranger smiles at another stranger in the street. Watch as people stop at stoplights.

All these are simple acts. And all of them express the better angels of our nature—we want to be helpful. We do ourselves a terrible disservice when we think otherwise.

But it's easy to fall into the habit of thinking people are just out for themselves. Why? There's a bunch of factors. The twenty-four-hour news cycle, so desperate to grab your attention, depends on the shock of people being despicable—the ultimate clickbait. Movies need tension— and what better drama than a crook or a villain? Yet day-to-day life is, by movie standards, pretty drama-free. It's just dads waking up and getting their kids ready for school. Social workers finding housing for the homeless. Coworkers bringing coffee to the team. No headlines there. Goodness is just too ordinary to grab anybody's attention. And yet. When practiced—when cultivated—it's life-changing.

Here's a little experiment to try. Just think of something sweet you did once. Like, for me, I helped a friend move. We had a great time together. And I smile when I think of it. No headlines, nobody even knows about it (except you now).

So what have you done in the last year that's pretty okay? Doesn't have to be big. Could be the smallest thing. You took a shift for your coworker. You sat up with a friend who was sad. Whatever. Now soak in that. Let your goodness sink in for a bit. And see how it feels.

Nice job. Next, think of something little *you could do* for someone else. Could be a kind word, a quick errand, a nice gift. You might send an email or a text. You might appreciate somebody. Or send good vibes. Now go do that thing.

Nobody likes a jerk. Being a jerk is a real downer. And we should really stop killing people—even online, even with words—if we want to live a happy life free of the hot mess–making madness of our questionable habits. And, by the way, we actually have choices. Every moment we have a choice. Kind of like flipping between radio stations. We can choose to remain like a block of wood for a minute, rather than blow a gasket. Better yet, we can choose to build kindness many times a day, every day, until kindness becomes our modus operandi, in such a way that we begin to be as helpful as possible, in a life-affirming upward spiral of glorious, glowing goodness untrammeled by . . . okay, you get the picture.

In any case, as we move along through these chapters, I think you'll find that the principles we're outlining—call them ethical guideposts, maybe—build, one upon another. Because here's the thing. For most of us, a lot of the reason it feels like the world is wildly unhinged is because we don't know—not really—what we stand for. Once we get unshakably clear about our own values, and once we get pretty good at using meditation to steady ourselves in that increasing clarity, then what other people do or think becomes a lot less crazymaking. Like the Buddha, we can learn to put our hand on the earth and say, "This is what I am about."

In that spirit, let's take a look at the next checkpoint. Because generosity is an essential building block of this semi-Buddhist survival guide for modern life.

GIVE A LITTLE

Devon

From a semi-Buddhist perspective, generosity is the very foundation of a decent life. Why? Well, for one thing, it's very nice to live in a social world constructed of mutually enriching and well-intentioned munificence. Compare that to a bunch of unhappy creeps always trying to take each other's stuff. Which would you choose? That's the obvious point.

Less obvious—and maybe even more important for our purposes—is that *generosity fills you up*. This concept is one of those beautiful semi-Buddhist paradoxes that it pays to remember when you're feeling bereft, discombobulated, and generally like a hot mess. Because when we give to others in wise ways, freely, of our own good wishes, that giving not only helps them; it helps us. As studies have shown, giving boosts your mood, improves your health, and makes you a generally more robust and joyful human.

But we'll get to all that. Let's start with the don'ts.

DON'T TAKE PEOPLE'S STUFF

The traditional Buddhist translation of this suggestion is "Don't take what's not freely offered." It's a bit clunky as a sentence, to be sure. But the clear message here is *don't steal*—don't take money out of your mom's purse; don't borrow the dress you know you won't return; definitely don't run a giant Ponzi scheme that bankrupts old ladies.

It seems obvious enough, doesn't it? One of those universal ethical guideposts just about any reasonable school of thought might abide. But, as with a lot of what we talk about in this book, when you start to look closely at your own life, it gets a little dicey.

For instance, for two years in my midtwenties I worked at a retreat center in the Colorado mountains. Long story short: I wasn't getting along perfectly with the founder. I thought she was a brilliant teacher, so gifted. But she was also my boss. And I was just not cool with her management style. Resentment began to build. And pretty soon I found myself doing something strange. The more annoyed I got with her, the more I started pilfering staples from the kitchen. Now, this was not exactly grand theft auto. But I knew that food wasn't for me. In fact, every time I swiped a handful of granola or some leftover soup, I felt guilty. But I didn't stop! I just rehearsed some silly rationalization to myself, stuffed down the guilt, and walked out with another few cups of dried lentils to cook in my cabin. The problem, of course, was that the more I did this, the more shaky I felt.

Looking back, I suppose the whole misguided fixation was some attempt to take back a little agency. What I actually did, though, was undermine myself. As the weeks went by, I felt less and less clear, more doubtful, more apprehensive. This little stealing, this knowing that I was not, in fact, upright in my values, blocked my ability to have the real (and difficult) conversations I needed to have with my boss.

Ultimately, stealing, even little-bitty stealing, undermines you. It saps your power. More than that, it reinforces the subtle sense that many of us secretly (and not so secretly) harbor that we don't have enough. We're somehow bereft, hungry. We just need that perfect life partner, that new iPhone, that cooler job—and then, finally, *then* we'll be happy.

But no. We get the life partner, the new phone, the job, but the craving mind continues. There is always another patch of very green grass over the next rolling green hill. And no matter how many hills we climb, there is always another hill, because if you look closely at your own mind, you knock up against the deeper truth that we, most of us, at least in post-capitalist, urbanized, techno-junky cultures, believe we *are not enough*.

Which is B.S. Total and complete bullshit.

But how do we start to deconstruct this ubiquitous tidal pull of inadequacy? Simple. We start by seeing the good.

SEE THE GOOD

When I met Craig, he'd been living at his Zen monastery in the remote mountains of southern Colorado for about five years. He had the shaved head, the black robes; he always smelled like fine Japanese incense. I loved a lot of things about him right off the bat—not least that he ran the kitchen and could throw together a meal for twelve by himself in less than an hour (hello? perk of a lifetime). But the thing that really caught my attention was the sign he had posted in his austere monk's quarters, right on the door so he'd notice it on the way out of his room. *See the good*, it said.

See the good. How many of us train our eye to see the good? How many of us train our ear to hear the good? And how often, in our daily rush of bad news, bad politics, and bad hair days, does the mind incline itself toward what's already good?

Let me ask another question: Did you know that most people, most of the time, actually treat each other pretty okay?

Soaked as we all are in the constant onslaught of the twenty-four-hour news cycle, pasting our eyeballs to the next terrible thing that's happening somewhere in the world, we forget that most people, most of the time, actually treat each other with relative care, with pretty decent okayness. Right now, people are yielding at yield signs. Right now, people are giving up their seats on the bus. Right now, mothers are loving their children. Right now, doctors are taking care of patients and shopkeepers are smiling at customers and people are giving to food banks and somewhere someone is meditating, letting their wholesome states of mind arise and flourish.

But did you know that Americans today think violent crime has risen in the past three decades?

And did you also know that violent crime has actually dropped in the last three decades?

The truth of the matter is that the world is all things—an incredibly complex, nearly hallucinogenic presencing of sights, sounds, thoughts, feelings, impressions, sensations—and our mind, this lightning-quick organizer of energetic influxes, makes sense of all this complexity with a handful of limiting but mostly useful shorthands that reduce it all into meaningful, workable sound bites.

But what if the mind is getting it wrong? More to the point, what if the mind is being duped by clickbait, by ad copy, by the pressurized insistence of a multinational media complex that needs you to look and look and look, and doesn't care a wit about how you feel about what you look at—as long as you just keep looking? And all this grasping for your attention ties right into a very human foible psychologists call *negativity bias.*

Have you heard about negativity bias? This is one of those classic psychology terms that, when you understand it and start to live the implications, can really change your life. Here's the deal:

Negativity bias is the simple but powerful idea that we, as humans, are more likely to see what's bad than what's good. Why? Most likely it's evolution. Evolution doesn't care whether you're happy. Evolution just cares whether you pass genes along. And so if you're living in a jungle with a bunch of attack cats and poisonous snakes, better to be on high alert all the time, and a little stressed out, than relaxed and happy and dead at sixteen.

Maybe all that made sense ten thousand years ago. But these days, with the advent of the information age, our negativity bias is continually enforced. You turn on the TV and there's a news report of some meaninglessly gruesome murder that happened in a quiet South Carolina town two thousand miles away. And then you go on Facebook and read about how the .01 percent are raking in huge dollars while the rest of us fight for scraps. And then you Netflix a bunch of crime shows and horror flicks and serial dramas where nothing ever resolves. And then you get an email about something going wrong at your job, and a text from your dad saying he's getting a CAT scan, and a friend sends you the latest apocalyptic account of what global warming might bring. And on and on and on. Which means your negativity bias is being confirmed and confirmed and confirmed and confirmed, until all you see when you look out at the world is people doing bad stuff and the planet going up in flames.

But here's the thing. As I just said: most people most of the time actually treat each other pretty okay. And though we are in the midst of an ecological crisis that needs to be addressed yesterday (or ten years ago), we can still train the mind to look, right now, in this present moment, at everything that is going *right*. Not because we are trying to fool ourselves. But because we have *already been fooled*, and we need to reset the focus and look with fresh eyes at what is already true so that we can build the resilience we'll need to address all the things that have to get done today, tomorrow, and for all the days after that. This process of resetting our focus, in fact, is how we sustain our energy in the face of the difficulties, setbacks, and betrayals that automatically accompany every worthwhile life endeavor.

It's actually not that hard, when you get into it. You just make small efforts all throughout the day to see the good, see the good, see the good. Reminding yourself to notice what's okay, what's wholesome, what's sweet, who's smiling, who's holding hands, who's taking care, and all the rest. Then, slowly, slowly, you start to see good everywhere. Kind of like buying a Toyota hatchback. Suddenly you just see Toyota hatchbacks on every little side street. Not because there's more on the road, obviously. But just because your eyes become attuned to their presence. With Toyota hatchbacks, this doesn't really matter all that much. But with negativity bias versus seeing the good it matters a whole lot. Why? Because the negativity bias makes us tight and small and scared. And seeing the good opens us up to all the good that's already right here in front of us and starts to prime us to find ways to be generous. Let's break this down into an easy-to-integrate daily practice.

A Little Meditation
SEE THE GOOD

The cool thing about this exercise is that after practicing this while sitting on a cushion or chair, you can take it out into your life and do it anywhere you are, anytime you want. I do this one a lot in my own life, while I'm riding the bus or walking to work, and it never fails to lift my mood, at least a little bit.

Step One: In Your Chair

Let's start this off sitting in a chair. As always, be comfortable. You want to strike a balance in your posture between alert and relaxed, but with a real lean toward relaxed. If you want, you can close your eyes between some of these sentences. Otherwise, just let your eyes go a little soft while you read. Now start to track your body. What are you feeling right now, in your chest and torso, your face and neck? See if you can release any tension that seems extra.

Now, from this semi-kind-of-relaxed state, think of something good. Could be anything. You love your cat. Perfect. You're finally single and it's awesome. Great. It's summertime. Let your mind run amok in goodness. Notice the littlest, funniest, happy-making things. And do this for at least five minutes.

Great! You have now seen the good. Don't worry if it was a struggle. Don't worry if nothing happened. We're just building habits here. We're not enlightened yet.

Step Two: On the Move

Now that you've accomplished seeing the good in your chair, it's time to take it on the road. If you want, you can write this down—write "See the Good" on a sticky note and leave it on your desk or bathroom mirror. And then when you remember, orient your mind toward what's going well in that moment.

Then try to do this at least three times in the next twenty-four hours. You can start right now. You're reading this book, and that's good! Or maybe you are sitting somewhere comfortable or drinking yummy tea. There is good in this moment.

It's helpful to do this at the beginning of the day, and also at the end. When you wake up, take stock of something positive. And before you fall asleep, notice one thing that is going well for you.

Throughout the day, you can pause when you remember, and see the good. Maybe you just finished a delicious breakfast. Or you're gonna be on time to your first meeting. Or your girlfriend just got a promotion.

You can orient toward the good as often as you'd like. And remember: there's no need to push or control things here. You might not feel that much as you notice someone's smile, receive a timely email, or write out a thank-you card. Remember that we're training an attitude, not so much a feeling.

Step Three: Don't Fool Yourself

One important caveat: "seeing the good" doesn't negate the difficult. We're not asking you to become some kind of Miss Pollyanna Sunshine who can't stand to have a tough conversation. We're simply balancing the negative with the positive in our lives, so that we don't get weighed down by what's challenging. Just take stock of what's good in you and what's good in those around you. And then see what happens. You might just find yourself more resourced, a tiny bit more whole, maybe even more ready to give a little.

GIVING FEELS GOOD

Okay, so far in this chapter we've talked about not taking people's stuff and seeing the good. Now we get to the best part: giving. Like I mentioned in the opening of this chapter, Buddhism tends to look at giving as the very foundation of a decent life. Not only does generosity ease up some of our calcified habits around wanting, which is a major reason we're a hot mess, it's also just plain fun. It brightens the mind and lightens the heart. It connects you with others. It boosts your self-worth. It's all-around just about my favorite thing.

But let's be honest: giving can actually be kind of hard. Sometimes I read stuff like this and I think, "Great, I'll just go ahead and give more." Then I end up running into all my stinginess, the tight little pockets of contraction, the *I can'ts* and *maybe-not-right-nows*—and then I feel bad about myself. Which is so obviously not the point.

So just to be clear: I'm not saying generosity is easy. And I'm not saying if you're a little stingy, like I sometimes am, that you should become Mother Teresa overnight. But what I am saying is that we can *train the mind to give.* How? Three simple steps.

1. Convince yourself.
2. Try a generosity meditation.
3. Start giving.

So the first step, convince yourself. Before you kick off any new, oh-so-healthy habit, whether it's exercise or veganism or random acts of kindness, you'll need to first put all (or at least most) of your doubts to rest. And one great way to TKO your doubts is by hitting them hard with science. Here are just a few findings to start us off:

- Generous people are healthier.[1]
- Generous people live longer.[2]
- Generous people are generally happier.[3]
- Your blood pressure actually drops when you give a gift.[4]
- Giving reduces stress.[5]
- Just a single act of generosity boosts your mood.[6]
- Simply thinking about giving can really improve your day.

Pretty convincing, right? Who doesn't want to live longer and healthier and happier with lower blood pressure and better moods? Let's drill down into one study[7] done at the University of British Columbia, which features a bunch of undergrads who were, unsurprisingly, split into two groups.

The first group was put through a battery of tests and

then given twenty dollars. They were told to go out and spend the money any way they wanted—as long as they spent it on themselves.

The second group was put through that same battery of tests and also given twenty dollars. The difference? They were told to go out and spend the money any way they wanted—as long as they spent it on others.

Any guesses on what happened next?

As expected, the undergrads who were given money to spend on themselves came back pretty happy.

But the undergrads who had been directed to spend money on others came back mega-boosted. They saw significant gains in mood, optimism, social connectivity, and other measures. And they couldn't stop telling the researchers about how excited they were to go back to their dorms and start handing out gifts to their friends.

So generosity can seriously boost your mood. Good to know, right? If you're feeling down, buy a little something for someone else. Recent studies have confirmed that the amount you spend doesn't matter—it truly is the thought that counts.

Okay, now that we've established that generosity really is good for you (you're convinced, right?), how do we get ourselves to actually do it? This is where meditation comes in. It's not enough to just believe something is good. We need to train the mind. In a way, this is no different from training muscles in the body. This generosity meditation is like training the gift-giving muscles of the mind.

A Little Meditation
GENEROSITY

Let's practice some generosity together. It'll be fun. Obviously you can't close your eyes while you're reading. But you can let yourself drop into a meditative state by slowing down, pausing, maybe even shutting your eyes between sentences as you try this little exercise on for size.

Step One

Imagine a time when you gave something. Make it a time when you gave something genuine. Not just the obligatory bottle of wine when you went to somebody's house or the birthday present that you secretly dug out of your "regift" box and then handed over to your unsuspecting friend who likely didn't want the State Farm baseball cap, either.

No, imagine a time when you offered a gift that meant something—both to you and to the person you gave it to. Maybe not an expensive something. Maybe not a thing at all. Maybe you did some babysitting for some friends who really needed a date night. Maybe you helped your buddy study for a test. Or maybe you got your sweetie tickets to Bruno Mars.

Doesn't matter what. Just as long as it's meaningful.

Now imagine what it was like to pick out the gift. Some joy there, maybe. Thinking about what this other person would really want. Going to the trouble of getting it. Spending the money or spending the time.

And now think of this person receiving the gift. Assuming it's one of those times when you hit the nail on the head—maybe their face lit up, or they actually jumped for joy. Perhaps hugs or high fives were exchanged.

Step Two

Imagine giving a gift in the future. Again, make it something genuine. Something you'd really love to give. Skipping, for now, the obligatory Mother's Day card or the housewarming knick-knack. Stay with something meaningful, something a friend or a loved one would really love to receive.

Again, this gift could be a thing. Or it could be a favor, a service, a meal, a kind word. There are so many different kinds of gifts. Just make sure it matters. And because this is in the future, it can also be imaginary, so you don't have to limit yourself. If your mom has always wanted to ride on a private jet, imagine getting her that ride. And then really get into imagining the smile on her face, the delight in her eyes, as she rises above the clouds with a glass of champagne in her hand and . . . you get the idea. Be specific. And really let your mind go for the details.

Step Three

Give something. Right now. Don't wait. It could be anything. No matter how small. But find some way to give something in this very moment. That's right. Put this book down. And . . . send somebody a text about how much you really appreciate them, or walk into the next room and hug your kids, or go online and one-click on a gag gift for a dear friend. Doesn't matter what you do. Just give. And stay with the meditation, continuing to notice how it feels in your body and mind as you do all this. Then come back and we'll close out with a final step.

Step Four

Track your response. Okay, you just remembered giving a gift, thought about giving a gift, and then actually gave a small gift. Now, just for a moment, check in with the area around your chest and throat. How is your breathing? Did it speed up or slow down during this meditation? Do you feel more relaxed? Or maybe more tight? Is there some sense of emotional warmth? Or maybe a kind of numbness, even resistance? Whatever comes alive for you is perfectly fine. Just use your mindfulness to track the response, take it as data, and maybe come back to the meditation a few times to see if things develop and change as you go. Ultimately, we're looking to tap the inherent joy of giving. But it might take a while to step your way up into that.

GIVE IN SMALL WAYS

The real truth of the matter is that you give all the time. You probably don't spend a lot of time paying close attention to the ways in which you give. This is an important point. Because psychologists have long known that attention holds a kind of power. In terms of good habits, what we give attention to flourishes. What we ignore, withers. And the very opposite is true of bad habits—those things we wish we didn't do, but still keep on doing. When we ignore them, they grow in the shadows, but when we face them with confidence and kindness, they can't stand up to the light of awareness for long. This is mindfulness. And this is the magnifying glass of concentrated awareness: the more we pay attention to the ways we are already generous, and note the physical sensations of how good it feels, the more that helpful habit will grow.

The good news is, you can practice generosity everywhere you go. For example, I spend a lot of time in airports traveling from one retreat center to another. Airports are not always the most relaxing places for me. I come from a family of nervous travelers, and no matter how many times I go through a TSA checkpoint, there is always some part of me that is scared I left something behind, or that I will somehow miss my plane, or misplace my wallet, or whatever. By the time I get through security, I can sometimes feel addled, or rattled, or just plain irritable.

But I've discovered a special antidote. First, I find a Starbucks or a Jamba Juice or whatever. Then I wait in line. I say hi to the cashier. And instead of buying myself something, I buy a gift card for five or ten dollars and leave it at the register to pay for the next few customers' drinks.

And then, just like that, I feel lighter, sweeter, happier. And I start to see the good again. I see all the ways others are being generous to each other all around the airport—fathers holding babies, mothers buying food for their kids, teenagers sharing earbuds, friends picking up the tab.

For me, that's all it takes. I spend at least an hour or two smiling.

But don't take my experience as proof. Try it out for yourself. Notice what happens when you practice generosity in real time. I admit, it might be a little awkward at first. A lot of habits feel awkward at first. That's why we need to practice them until they become second nature.

AND ANOTHER THING...
Set Clear Boundaries

Before we go any further, this is probably a good moment to tap the brakes and say a few things that need to be said. So far I've been framing generosity as a simple, unadulterated good—just go ahead and do this and your life will get better. And that's true, of course.

But there's a problem. And that problem is that some people in our culture get some messages and other people get other messages. Like, if you're a white man raised in the middle class who went to good public schools and then a grand old ivy-covered college, you've been told, more or less, "The world is yours, build your dreams, oysters, etc."

But. If you are anything but a white man raised in the middle class, then you've likely gotten a whole different set of messages. Even if you're a white woman raised in the middle class who went to good public schools and all the rest, the messages you've likely received sound a lot more like, "Take care of everyone else before yourself, please others, especially white men, and look amazing doing it."

Or if you're a black man or woman or an Asian American trans kid, the messages are even more destructive still.

So without going into all the details of all the sociological and psychological and economic subtle-and-not-so-subtle pressures that each of us lives with and lives through, this is just a note to say, "Don't do stuff that's bad for you."

Let me repeat that: *Don't do stuff that's bad for you.*

For example, apropos of the last chapter ("Don't Be a Jerk"). Let's say you're really helpful to someone. Say you're nonbinary and he's a man, just for fun. And then let's say that, after you're helpful to this person once, twice, three times, he turns around and treats you like dirt, walks all over you, talks behind your back, alienates your friends, clears out your bank account, keys your car, and stamps out your spirit.

Are we telling you to continue to be helpful to this person?

Of course not.

Likewise with this chapter ("Give a Little"). And likewise with every chapter. We are not asking you to give and give and give and give and give some more until you are a paper-thin wisp of your former self, exhausted, aggravated, and helpless, blown by the endless storms of the world, unarmored in the midst of the inevitable catastrophes of everyday life.

That's not what we're saying at all. If you're actually going to be helpful to all the rest of us, we need you to set good boundaries, get enough sleep, find time to exercise, spend evenings with friends, just freakin' relax, and all the rest of it. You can't be *on* all the time, even when things are going well. And if things are going badly, or someone is taking advantage of you, then you'll need to armor up and set things straight. No two ways about it.

But how?

Well, take the above example of the dude you've been nice to who talks behind your back and walks all over you. We've already established that what you *don't* do is let him continue to treat you like dirt, alienate your friends, etc.

But what *do* you do?

One option—a favorite of so many of us—is to turn around and treat *him* like dirt, walk all over him, talk behind his back, key his car, and on and on. Or just assassinate him on social media. But what we're recommending in this book is a more balanced approach. A return to civility. You'll be firm, yes. You'll make damn sure he stops his B.S. this minute. But you won't destroy him. And you won't need to, because once you get good at this kind of boundary setting, you'll do it early and often, and dudes like that will know better than to mess with you.

So the basic message here is: please don't take people's stuff. It's bad for them, and bad for you. Also, instead of drowning in bad news, try seeing the good. When you see the good—in yourself, in others—you begin to fill up with a sense of joyful purpose. Once you're really filled up like that, it's easier to give a little, and once you get into giving, it becomes a kind of upward spiral of mutually reinforcing beneficence. Not to mention lower blood pressure and all that. But don't be a pushover, either. Set boundaries when you need to.

By now you may have noticed that we think there are some core semi-Buddhist principles that will guide you well as you begin this process of living through your values. These start with not killing people (or assassinating them on Twitter). From there, you could instigate the delightful but slow process of building kindness, heartfulness, and (in this chapter) generosity—not in a sappy way, but in a feet-planted-firmly-on-this-earth sort of way. Where you really show up for your life, moment after moment, consciously, clearly (see chapter 6), and without excuses. Where you commit to helping yourself and helping others. You know, like Batman. But without the cape and without kicking people's teeth in all the time.

So what's next? you might ask. What's next is a deeper dive into the world of speech, because how we speak stands at the very heart of this survival guide.

SAY WHAT'S TRUE

Craig

Imagine a world in which people told the truth. Always. As a matter of course. In this world, every politician who gave a speech would meticulously attune themselves to the facts, and be careful to say only the clearest, cleanest essence of their actual understanding. Every time you went to a mechanic, in this imagined world, you'd never worry about whether they were overcharging you, about whether you really actually needed that new air filter. In your relationship, your partner would be real with you, telling you what was on their mind and in their heart, so you'd know exactly where you were standing in that loving encounter, every day of the year.

How does that sound? Well, for some people it might sound a little terrifying. Some of us are not quite ready to hear the truth, especially from our loved ones. But for most of us, I think, there is a deep longing for this kind of world. It seems that every time we turn on the TV we're confronted with mendacity, half-truths, outright lies, and sly little innuendos. Politicians are lying to us. Corporations are lying to us. Advertising is just one big bold-faced never-ending lie. And, for some of us, even our loved ones can't seem to get it together to tell us what's really going on.

Into this whirlwind of prevarication and shallow weaselliness, I offer you the Buddha's fourth recommendation for surviving modern life while the whole world spins off its collective axis: don't lie.

BUT WE ALL LIE!

Don't lie. Seems simple enough, right? And yet, it is devilishly hard to get through a whole day without lying at least once. And most of us can't even get through an hour without telling multiple half-truths, obfuscations, and all-out falsehoods. As recent studies have shown.

For example, if you conduct an online survey—as a group of researchers did recently—only about 40 percent of respondents admit they've lied in the last twenty-four hours.[1]

But if you actually watch people in conversation, as another group of researchers did, about two-thirds of our fellow humans can't go *ten minutes* without telling a lie.[2]

In fact, by one estimate, a quarter of our friends under forty lie on their resumes.[3] Nine out of ten people lie on their dating profiles.[4] And the forty-fifth president of the United States lied bigly 2,140 times just in his first year in office.[5]

Which brings us to the obvious question—why shouldn't you lie?

Besides the obvious reason, which is that the world would be a better place and we'd all be a lot more relaxed and happy if everyone told the truth. No, even given that the world will probably not become a more honest place any time soon and everyone will continue on with their fibbing ways, why shouldn't *you* lie?

Well, here are three reasons, each one backed by research.

First, *lying is stressful.*[6] Research done over the past twenty years points to a pattern most of us are probably familiar with. It goes like this:

- When we tell the truth, we simply remember what we said.[7]
- Remembering what we said reduces our cognitive load and we can use those neural resources for other stuff, like solving problems, regulating emotions, and relating skillfully to others.
- When we lie, though, we need to continually rehearse to ourselves the lie we've told so we remember to tell it the same way again later.
- Rehearsing to remember our lies takes up a lot of headspace. And it's stressful.

All of this is no big deal if you're just lying one time because some grad student in a white coat told you to. But if you're lying in real life, your lies don't stay in the lab. They follow you. You've got to keep things straight, and you've got to remember who you said what to, and you've got to make sure you don't get caught.

Second, *lying kills your reputation.* Again, the research has a lot to tell us here. For example, one study conducted at Northwestern University's Kellogg School of Management[8] followed business students over the course of a semester as they learned to negotiate. During that time, the students in the class earned reputations as "liars," "tough but fair," or "cream puffs." Then the researchers watched as the students entered into negotiations with one another in the final week of the semester. Far and away, the students who had earned reputations as liars fared the worst. Their fellow students treated them the most aggressively, were least polite to them, and offered them fewer concessions.

Third, lying is *literally bad for your (mental and physical) health.* A few years ago a group of researchers at Notre Dame conducted a study in which they split participants into two groups. Both groups came in once a week and—while hooked up to a lie detector—answered questions about how often they'd lied in the previous week. The difference between the groups? One group was given tips on how to avoid lying during the week. The other group wasn't.

Both groups actually saw the numbers of lies they told drop throughout the study. But the first group—the one with the truth training—told a whole lot fewer lies. And the researchers found that the ones who lied less saw improvements in their physical and mental health. They also had less trouble sleeping, saw improvements in their relationships, had fewer headaches and less overall tension. They even reported fewer sore throats.

All this positive fallout comes down to what the Buddha called "the bliss of blamelessness." Put simply, when you come to the end of your day, and you put your cell phone on airplane mode and put your head down on your pillow, if you can look back on everything you said, and everything you did, and see that you didn't lie, cheat, steal, or kill, you'll feel less bad.

This feeling good will make it easier to sleep. It will also make sex better (yes, really, and we'll get to that in the next chapter), and it will be a heck of a lot easier to sit down and meditate, if that's what you choose to do.

Okay, so just don't lie. When somebody asks you a question, answer it straight. When you need something, ask for it straight. In fact, every time you open your mouth to say something in this great spinning world of interpersonal ups-and-downs, just say what's true. And don't say what's not true. And that's it.

OR AT LEAST KNOW YOUR LIES

Again, not lying seems simple enough, right? And yet, after just about twenty-five years of trying my level best to uphold this slippery little ethical guidepost, I am sorry to report that it certainly hasn't been easy for me.

To be sure, I rarely tell outright lies at this point. But, still, I notice myself bending facts a little here, trimming the truth just a bit over there. And, man, I tell you, when it comes to exaggeration, I just can't seem to get a handle on my mouth.

Like, if the fish was ten inches, I'll say it was twelve (not that I fish, but you get the picture). Or if the traffic was backed up three miles, I'll say it was four. And if I'm telling a story about someone I admire, their good qualities become larger than life.

I'm told this tendency toward hyperbole is because I'm a Sagittarius, and so I just can't help myself. Everything is larger than life for me. I don't know anything about astrology, but I can tell you it's a little embarrassing when my wife, or my brother Mark, or someone who knows me well, looks at me sideways and says, "Really? The traffic was backed up four miles?" And then I have to think it through and realize, no, it was more like three miles. Okay, two and a half, but it *felt like forever.*

At any rate, exaggeration is a kind of lying, and as I've held this thought of *say what's true* for myself over the years, I've noticed more and more how even this seemingly little excursion from the facts carries with it a slight loss in trust, a tiny little break in communication. And so I try to watch myself and say what's *truly* true so I can have the kinds of intimate relationships I want and live a life I feel mostly really good about.

Okay. So. Lying. Is. Bad. Don't do it. Or at least try not to do it. Now you're just going to walk around telling the absolute truth all the time to everyone you meet, friend or stranger, bus driver or boss, right? Well, here's a caveat.

SAY WHAT'S TRUE (BUT NOT ALWAYS)

Now I will admit something embarrassing. For years—and I mean years—I suffered from the inexpedient assumption that I should really tell people what was on my mind. No matter whether it was good or bad, friendly or unfriendly, or just plain irrelevant. Where did I get this ridiculous idea?

Well, there have been a series of psychotherapies and philosophies, most of them rooted in some bad Freudian provocations, many of them finding their greatest reach and impact in the 1960s and '70s, which stated, more or less: *speak your mind*. These systems of conduct valued authenticity above all. They derided society's scripted interactions. They sought to liberate their followers from the oppression of everyday propriety and release them into a realm of personal, sexual, and relational candor, an ever-expanding adventure of self-expression and life-as-art joy.

Or that was the idea. What actually happened, at least for me, was I ended up telling people a bunch of nonsense that was in my head, free of the context of those experimental social movements, and ended up in all manner of trouble. I could list about a hundred times when I did this, each more knuckleheaded than the last. But let me just give you a quick and easy (and fairly minor) example.

Last year, Devon and I celebrated our wedding anniversary. It happened to be right before we were making a big move to Hawai'i so I could do my clinical work and finally finish my PhD. It also happened to coincide with an absolute apex of the migrant detainment epidemic at the Mexican-American border, with daily news reports of children locked in cages and families broken up and re-processed and sometimes never finding their way back to each other. So when my dear mother bought us an anniversary gift—a beautiful, though breakable, vase—I said to her, "Hey, how about we return this vase that we can't really take with us to Hawai'i and donate the proceeds to the Refugee and Immigrant Center for Education and Legal Services (RAICES), since they're doing such good legal work at the border."

Now, my dear mother had just gone through a breakup with her longtime boyfriend (don't worry, they got back together) and also just retired and also just moved, and she was in no mood to be told that the lovely vase she'd bought us could not be transported to Hawai'i and that, anyway, wouldn't it be better to put all that money toward do-gooding? So she kind of got pissed. And I apologized. And she said, "You know, sometimes it's just better to lie. If only by omission."

That's a lesson I'm still trying to learn. Not to lie, really. But to know when to keep my mouth shut. Thankfully, a really long time ago, the Buddha offered a bunch of good advice on how to do just that. In fact, all those years ago, he didn't just say, "Say what's true," he actually gave a handy-dandy list of questions to ask ourselves before we say anything at all.

TRUE, KIND, TIMELY, HELPFUL

Unlike the proto-Freudian hedonists of the human potential movement, with their utopian ideals of interpersonal authenticity, the Buddha actually recommended that we be pretty careful with our speech. In fact, he devoted a substantial portion of his substantial teachings to advising people about how to speak to each other. There could be whole books on the topic, in fact. (And there are.) But for our purposes we can sum up the Buddha's advice in four simple questions. Questions you can ask yourself just before you open your mouth to say something—anytime, to anyone.

Is This True?

Is what I'm about to say true? Am I speaking the truth? Is what I'm saying clear and honest? Or am I bending things in some way? Am I spinning, pushing the truth a bit, massaging the facts to get something I want out of this interaction?

If the answer to any of these questions is anything but "Yup, this is true," then the Buddha advises that you don't speak. Instead, take a moment, hold your tongue, and consider other options.

Is This Kind?

Is what I am about to say kind? Is what I am about to fire off in this text or email considerate? Is this heated missive in an online forum caring? Is it taking into account the other person's inner world? Even when that other person might be a loved one who has seriously pissed me off, or a total stranger who so obviously seems to deserve a whopping verbal punch in the proverbial face?

Again, if the answer to any of these questions is anything other than "Yes, what I am about to say is kind," then the Buddha advises silence. Take a minute. Think things through. Is there a way to say this that's kind? Or at the very least, not unkind? Ninety-nine out of a hundred times there is a way. You just have to find it. And once you start to realize how much less your life feels like it's spinning out of control when you start to interact this way, you'll be more and more motivated to try.

Is It Timely?

Is what I am about to say timely? Is this the right time to say this? If it's eleven o'clock at night and your boyfriend/girlfriend/significant other is about to fall asleep, is this the right time to bring up that thing that happened at eleven o'clock this morning and has been kind of troubling you, but not really that much, but actually, well, kind of a lot? I'm not saying it would definitely be the wrong time. But you could think it through. Might there be another time to bring this up honestly and kindly that would better serve the conversation?

Is It Helpful?

So these words are about to leave my mouth. Quick check: Are they actually helpful? Are they going to move the situation forward in the way I want? How will they land for the person (or people) in front of me?

Sometimes, for sure, it's hard to know what's helpful and what's not. And it's definitely tough to know just exactly how something will land for the people in our lives. But one surefire way to get it right a lot more of the time is to at least make sure your *intention* is to be helpful.

SKILLFUL SPEECH

There are people out there—and I've met a lot of them now—who follow these guidelines of True, Kind, Timely, Helpful beautifully. And they all have some things in common: they have good friends, stable community connections, a sort of quiet confidence, and they kind of glow.

There are, therefore, a lot of great examples I could offer. But the one I know best is my wife, Devon. Devon beams goodness at everyone she meets. When we go jogging together, for example, she smiles at every person we pass. Not in that awkward, socially conventional, I'm-smiling-because-I'm-supposed-to kind of way. It's more like she's saying, *I'm so glad we share this planet together.*

And you should see people's reactions. I've seen strangers do a double take. They've stopped walking and just stood, basking in that sunlight. Nearly everyone smiles back. And when they do, it's a real smile, the smile of recognition and connection.

For another instance, a while back I worked on the Hawaiian island of Moloka'i, three days a week, for a year.

Moloka'i is known as an outer island. It's small, with a population of about 7,500, about 60 percent Native Hawaiian. To say the community there is tight-knit would be an understatement. Folks hold an air of skepticism; outsiders are treated as just that—outsiders. So when, after three months, I had been pretty well accepted into the community as a therapist, I felt relieved and happy.

Then Devon came for a visit from where we were living on O'ahu. Within days she was a local favorite. The woman in the coffee shop, who had only warmed up to me after months, warmed up to Devon within minutes. The food-truck folks, the bartender at the restaurant, random people on the street—within days people knew Devon and treated her like a welcome friend.

The thing is, though, this level of radiant presence doesn't just come naturally. Or part of it does. But the other part has to do with training. Devon has been refining her own mind, day after day, year after year, on and off the meditation cushion. She has been paying careful attention to her interactions with others, checking in again and again to see how things go whenever she turns herself to the world. Also, I know for a fact that she's always asking herself the same elementary questions I listed above: True? Kind? Timely? Helpful? And this allows her to show up and be more fully attuned to the range of people in her life.

Now, of course, I'm not saying Devon never stumbles. In the ten years we've been together I've seen her make hardcore social errors, embarrass herself, embarrass others (including me), step on people's toes, and even occasionally tick off the innocent bystander. So what we don't want to do is make this into some rigidly unattainable goal of theatrical smoothness. Devon is a work in progress; me, too; you, too: everybody's just stumbling through together, trying to figure it all out. The key is to start checking your mind. What are you thinking? Could it be slightly truer, kinder, and the rest? Then check the words that are about to leave your lips. The more you say what's true and kind and timely and helpful, the more the world will begin to become a friendlier place.

A Quick Meditation
SPEAK WISELY

Let's try to bring some awareness to how you communicate with others. By recognizing times when you've been honest and upright in speech, you gain confidence in your ability to hone this skill. It's really possible, though not always easy. And while it can take time, the payoff is totally worth it. So let's practice this with a little formal meditation.

Get comfy. Breathe deeply a few times and let your nervous system relax and settle. Spend a few moments just feeling the moment and being okay as you are.

Now think of a time when you really spoke skillfully. A time when you were honest and kind, and your speech was timely and useful. Maybe you spoke truth to power. Or you confessed something to your significant other and it deepened your intimacy. Or you wrote a clear email at work. It doesn't have to be blown-away amazing speech, just a time when you felt good about how you communicated. Maybe it wasn't easy to tell the truth, but you did anyway.

Once you've picked your moment, spend some time remembering it as if it's happening right now. Remember your words and how your body felt as you spoke them or emailed them or texted them or sexted them. You don't have to feel all glowy here; just stay curious about how wise speech feels when you do it.

Okay, great. Now let go of the reflection and relax for a few moments. Simply be with your body and your mind as they are. Nice work. You're done. Feel free to come back to this exercise from time to time. I've gone through periods where I've done something like this every day for a week or two, just to get a handle on the stuff that's coming out of my mouth.

YES, YOU CAN STILL BE STERN

So now that you've reflected on talking with honesty and heard about my wife (yes, by the way, I know I'm highly biased), I'm hoping you're inspired to try following the Buddha's guidelines for speech: True, Kind, Timely, Helpful. But if you're anything like me, you're probably also wondering, *Am I just going to have to try to walk around with a buttery smile all over my face like I've had some kind of a ketamine lobotomy? What about when people do stupid stuff, dangerous stuff, mean stuff? Am I supposed to let them walk all over me and just be Zen about it?*

As we've mentioned already: of course not. Some of the kindest people I know can also be the fiercest. Remember Dr. Bonnie Duran back in chapter 2. Remember our whole disquisition about setting boundaries in chapter 3. And, just for kicks, let me describe another example of a preternaturally kind and compassionate human being who also engages in some serious straight talk.

There is a Tibetan teacher we studied with in Hawai'i named Lama Rinchen. In the year that we were with him, Lama Rinchen was eighty-eight years old, a small, quiet man with a quiet voice who was always smiling and calm. As an ordained Buddhist monk, he wore his same red robes every day, day after day. He ate simple food, lived in the temple where we all came to study, and spoke to whomever showed up in the same calm, even tone. Lama Rinchen is, as far as I am concerned, a true Buddhist adept, a master of his own mind who seems to never lose his cool and, unlike me, never wavers from the sort of kind, lighthearted presence that we might think of as saintly.

Until one day. Because in the center where Lama Rinchen teaches there was a longtime student, whom I'll call William. And William was always making trouble. He was disdainful of other students, haughty about his Buddhist textual knowledge, and above all, very, very confident in his high levels of spiritual attainment.

So on this one fresh summer Sunday morning in the hills above Honolulu, we all did our ninety-minute group practice together, as we did every Sunday. And after the practice, Lama Rinchen asked if anyone had questions, as he did every Sunday. And a student raised her hand and asked a question about the unborn nature—a very high-level question about our experiential knowing of absolute reality.

Lama Rinchen paused. As he was gathering his thoughts to answer in his quiet, kind, somewhat broken English, William turned around and began to unfurl a haughty disquisition on the unborn nature. On and on he went. Lama Rinchen simply watched him go. The room full of students simply watched him go. If people were upset, no one seemed to show it. When William took a breath, the student who had asked the question gently interrupted him, in a way that I found both skillful and firm. She said, "Thank you, William, but I was actually asking Lama Rinchen to answer this question."

William shrugged, as if to say, *Well, I can answer it faster and better.* Then he was quiet for a moment.

The whole room turned to Lama Rinchen, who began, slowly, meticulously, to give an extraordinarily subtle explanation of the unborn nature, based entirely on textual reference, but shot through with his own deep, decades-long meditation experience. Things were going great, until, again, he stopped for a moment to collect his thoughts, and William jumped in again. And this time he *corrected* Lama Rinchen! Never mind that Lama Rinchen ordained at the age of twelve and studied with the greatest masters of Tibet before coming to the West. Never mind that Lama Rinchen has spent years in cloistered meditation retreat. And never mind that William's correction was technically inaccurate—he just launched into his own explanation, all over again, of the unborn nature.

Now the room was getting tense. Someone interrupted William and asked him, "Why don't you let Lama Rinchen finish?"

Again, William shrugged, as if to say, *Sure, but I know this stuff better.*

"Or maybe you want to teach us all today?" Lama Rinchen said, smiling quietly.

William didn't get the joke. He began to launch once more into his lecture.

But this time Lama Rinchen had had enough. "William," he said. And when William looked up, Lama Rinchen said, very slowly, in the same calm, kind, quiet voice he always uses, "you know nothing about the dharma," the Buddha's teachings.

William began to protest, but now Lama Rinchen interrupted him. "Books," he said, "books, books, books, you know all the books. You have read all the books. Books aren't dharma. Dharma is here," Lama Rinchen said, pointing at his own heart. "Dharma is only here. Where is your heart, William? Talking, talking, always talking, look what you have talked yourself into."

Then Lama Rinchen, who had known William for many years, got personal. "You have destroyed your family," he said quietly, calmly. "Two little girls. Can't even see them. Wife won't talk to you. Friends won't talk to you. Your business is destroyed. Why?" Lama Rinchen said. "Because you're talking, talking, talking. Dharma is all up here for you," Lama Rinchen said, pointing to his own head. "But here, in the heart: arrogance. William knows, William always knows. William knows everything. Except how to live a dharma life."

William stormed out of the center, calling Lama Rinchen a fool and a fake. After he had gone, Lama Rinchen turned to all of us and continued to answer the question.

Now, let me ask you, was what Lama Rinchen said true? Dead-on. Not a hint of exaggeration. Nor, for that matter, did he pull any punches. He said it exactly as he saw it.

Was what Lama Rinchen said kind? It certainly wasn't sweet or accommodating. But from a Buddhist perspective, and this was clearly his intention, what he said was the central act of kindness. He saw that William, with his arrogance and gruffness, was creating terrible situations for himself. And he tried to help by forcefully pointing it out.

Was it timely? I think so. William was verbally crashing around the dharma hall, making it pretty hard for the rest of us to learn anything. He was also, in his own life outside the building, creating untold and unnecessary suffering for himself and everyone else. The time to say something was right then.

And was what Lama Rinchen said helpful? This is always a tough one. What I can say with total certainty, however, is that what Lama Rinchen said was *intended* to be helpful, both to William and to all the rest of us in the room. He was trying with great care to show us all how to live a decent life.

So you see, saying what's true, and kind, and timely, and helpful doesn't have to mean walking around like a big melting ball of mashed potatoes. It can mean being stern and forceful—but with the intention to truly benefit the situation, and even the jerky jerk in the room.

NOW RELAX

A lot of folks who encounter these teachings—well-meaning people, with good hearts, so earnest—can get very uptight. They can start to get exceedingly vigilant about their own speech. I've seen this many times with my dharma friends. It's like they start to make these guidelines into epic rules. They apply these rules all over the place, to everything they say, and then to everything everyone else says, too.

At the same time, speech is a complex territory. A choppy ocean. It is, in fact, at the heart of the heart of the storm of our contemporary world. So what we want to do is keep a relaxed eye on our speech, lightly using these suggestions— and they're just suggestions—as a way to make fewer unnecessary problems for ourselves as we navigate the hot mess of human beings talking to each other every day.

In this endeavor, we can apply the mindfulness that we've been developing in our meditation practice. Just as we bring a warm awareness, a kind attention, to our breath, we can bring a patient, continual attention to our speech. I've found that the body is a good barometer. When we're saying something skillful, our bodies feel relaxed and good. And when we're lying or blabbering or mouthing off, our bodies feel tight and hot and not-so-good. You can use this body awareness to tell you when you're on or off track. You can also notice when what you've said was actually pretty well-intentioned but didn't go so well. Intention and impact are two different things. We learn from our mistakes—we have to—and practice humility and patience and ask for forgiveness when we do mess up. Asking for forgiveness is another form of wise speech, and it doesn't have to be all full of guilt and self-recrimination and apology. It's not all about you. Simply acknowledge your mistake and the impact it made, remember your decent intentions, and then do it differently next time.

So we can notice when we really get off track. You will get off track! Just know that. Everybody gets off track. But what starts to happen is that we get a little *less* off track, and then a little less, until finally we're on track, or pretty semi-close to on track, most of the time.

One of my teachers used to call this the fluorescent light bulb theory of enlightenment. Remember those old fluorescent light bulbs that, when you hit the light switch, would click on and off, then on and off, faster and faster, until what you saw was just a continual stream of clear light? (Okay, if you're under thirty you probably have no idea what I'm talking about.) Anyway, our experience with refining speech is a little like that. We do good, then not so good, then good again, then a big kerfuffle. But gradually, gradually, we get a little better and a little better and a little better as time goes on, until one day we look up and actually our life is way less hectic than it used to be. We're apologizing less for the dumb things we said. We're not constantly putting out fires. Our friends are, actually, pretty much never mad at us anymore. That's the capacity that we have to live a sane life right in the middle of the hot mess of the world without being such a hot mess ourselves.

So lying is bad. But we all lie. It's actually really hard to stop lying, but there are good reasons to try—like better relationships, less stress, and feeling good about yourself when you rest your head on your pillow every night. Still, we don't have to go on blathering about everything that traipses through our skull, either. In fact, the Buddha offered a framework for how to think about this in four questions: True? Kind? Timely? Helpful?

All that said, my observation is that speech—which we're doing, in one way or another, constantly, all day, every day— is right at the heart of the matter of bringing more sanity into your life. Or, in the reverse, making things that much more crazytown. Now, of course the world may continue to spin out and get messy and people may keep gossiping and criticizing and aggravating and undercutting. A lot of that might not change. But there is something just a little extraordinary that happens when you make a conscious decision to stick with these principles we've been talking about over the past bunch of pages. And this speech thing, especially, is huge. You can really start to shift things for yourself if you take this one to heart.

Next up, sex. Because actually the Buddha had a lot to say about sex. Okay, what Devon's going to say here is only very loosely based on what the Buddha actually said, to be sure. But I'd like to think that if the Buddha were alive today as a cisgender thirty-eight-year-old American nonmonastic woman, he'd say something a lot like what you're about to read.

5

MAKE SEX GOOD

Devon

Let's kick off this chapter with a quick contemplation about sex, shall we?

You can do this while you read but you might want to slow down a bit. Maybe take a brief pause after each question. Let it drop in, let it work on you. No need to come up with a clear or perfect answer. Just ask the question. Pause. Feel your body. And see what comes up.

Ready? Please get cozy, and take a few mindful breaths. Now ask yourself these questions:

- What is sex about, for me?
- What is my version of good, powerful, meaningful sex?
- How do my deepest values inform my sex life?
- How might my sex life express my deepest values?

Okay, how was that? Don't worry if you've got nothing. Maybe you feel blank and numb and weird inside. Or maybe you're flooded with a disorganized river of thoughts, images, memories, emotions. Or maybe you had a little insight. All those experiences are fine. The trick is, whatever's happening in the mind and heart and body—whether it's newfound clarity or a truckload of sludge and muck—just know it clearly, and keep knowing it, and see how it develops over time.

For me, I've been sitting with these questions my entire adult life. I certainly don't have all the answers. But I thought I'd share a few pieces of my own story and a couple of thoughts on where I believe we are, all of us, in this sociohistorical moment of highly sexualized global capitalist culture.

Which is to say, I'd like to start by talking about shame.

THE CHRISTMAS GIFT

I remember the first time I felt ashamed of my body. I was ten years old. It was Christmas. My parents, sweet and unsuspecting, handed me a wrapped gift in front of the sparkling tree, all lit up and hung with angels. I remember holding the package in my hands, knowing it was clothes of some kind. I remember the excitement as I carefully ran my fingers along the edge of the wrap, releasing the tape to reveal the flat rectangular red Macy's box inside. Then the elation as I lifted the top of the box and found a green cotton turtleneck—exactly what I'd wanted.

I jumped up, childish in my excitement. I hugged my mom, hugged my dad, ran upstairs to my room, stripped off my plaid pajama top and pulled the turtleneck on, fully expecting to be delighted by what I saw.

Instead, for the first time in my life, I was overcome with a sinking dread. The green turtleneck's cotton was skintight, clinging. When I looked in the mirror, I saw one thing and one thing only: my belly. Which was sticking out of the fabric like a huge round hateful blob.

I remember thinking I had done something despicable, something horribly wrong. And I remember thinking, for the first time in my life, "I'm fat." I will never forget the sense of spinning, of drowning, a sensation I would grow used to as I looked and looked and looked in the mirror, again and again, looking for something else, or someone else—some idea of myself—all throughout my teenage years.

A different kid would have simply tossed that brand-new skintight green turtleneck to the back of her ten-year-old closet and never worn it again. But I wasn't that kid. I made a different choice. Consciously, in front of the mirror that day, I decided I would suck in my belly and never let it out again.

Why is this story in a chapter about good sex? Put simply: sex is about being in a body. And if we're not allowed to be in our bodies, just exactly as they are, then we'll never have the kind of full-bellied, openhearted, super-sensual, mutually wonderstruck orgasms we've been dreaming of. Sex will just be, at best, another part of the day we check out of, like buying groceries or watching TV.

More than that, sex won't necessarily line up with our deepest values. Because, for me at least, it's not just about killer orgasms. (Which are great. I'm not knocking orgasms.) It's about living my values in my whole life: my work, my family, my friendships, my spirituality . . . and my sex. Which values? Well, I want to be alive in my body, using my body and heart and mind to recognize and express wisdom and compassion. I want to be alive with others. I want to be alive with myself. I want to be of benefit, fully engaged in all the areas of my life.

Maybe you want some version of this for yourself, too. But how do we make sex good? How do we make it whole and wholesome and embodied and frisky?

Well, first we have to look at what's getting in the way.

THE TRINITY OF BAD SEX: OBJECTIFYING. PATRIARCHAL. CONSUMERISM.

Back to the skintight green Christmas turtleneck. What was that about? Why would a ten-year-old (and I was a very innocent ten-year-old) have a semi–heart attack alone in her room just from putting on a turtleneck? Why would she fall to the depths of misery over her round (pretty adorable) belly, which, by the way was *not* big, *not* fat, and definitely *not* the result of some horrible, disfiguring lack of self-control or disordered eating. So where did this unshakable intuition come from, this absolute certainty that I *should be different*?

I blame patriarchy. Or more accurately, the adult me looks back on the ten-year-old me and I blame *objectifying patriarchal consumerism*.

Pretty complicated, huh?

Now, Craig and I promised ourselves we wouldn't get all academic and cultural studies in this book, so feel free to skip to the next section, "Take Back Your Body," if you're not into this stuff. But in this one instance, I do actually think we need a few big words to make a few big points. Because the dynamics that I want to talk about, the dynamics that need to be unpacked and unraveled and maybe even uprooted, are slippery. We need words that can stand up to their slipperiness and help us get a handhold, so that we can finally see clearly what our bodies and minds are being tasked with, and just say, "Nope."

Make sense? Okay then, let me take those three big words (*patriarchy*, *objectification*, *consumerism*) one at a time and break them down into their meaningful, useful parts. Because let's be real here: you cannot make sex good without first uprooting all the insidious ways our global media sell, sell, sell you into making sex bad. Which really translates into all the richness and complexity of human sexuality and sensuality having been squeezed into a power-infused, commodified, hedonistic, tight little package of . . . alienation.

Yeah, alienation. Ever felt super alone and kind of empty after sex? Keep reading.

Patriarchy, as I think of it, is the pervasive and largely undisputed, almost entirely unacknowledged assumption that men are first. Not that they are superior, necessarily—although that can be one flavor of firstness. But just simply that they are first, fundamental, the standard. First Adam, then Eve. First male presidents, then (someday, maybe) a woman. And when it comes to sex, it's often, first you, then me.

Patriarchy does lots of stuff. But the biggest thing it does is give some people (i.e., men) more power than others (i.e., women and people who are gender-nonconforming). It's a kind of service economy where one gender gets the goods, and the others provide the goods. This is a profoundly shitty arrangement for men, women, and those who don't fall easily into these categories because, as a way of being, unchecked male-firstness fundamentally disconnects us all from the possibility of real, nonhierarchical, loving relationships with each other, where pleasure is equally shared.

Objectification is a close cousin of patriarchy. It's the sense of looking at ourselves from outside our bodies. It's the surfacing of experience. The sense that we are always being looked at, always under the gaze of another, that even when we are alone in our room, we are somehow being examined, measured, rated. While this dynamic is most classically related to being a woman—and women have historically been more damaged by this sense of being under the microscope—the advent of social media, smartphones, selfies, and the incessant public chronicling of experience has made it an epically excruciating phenomenon from which no one escapes. And it's so utterly omnipresent that most people don't even know they are looking at themselves as if from outside themselves, continually performing their physicality for an invisible (or often visible) impersonal lens.

Still with me? Great, then let's talk *consumerism*. Which is a largely undisputed two-pronged idea: first, that stuff will make us happy, and second, that people are just part of the stuff that can serve to make us happy.

The idea that stuff will make us happy, of course, is nothing new. Humans have been acquiring and treasuring stuff ever since there was stuff to acquire and treasure. But with mass production and worldwide economic growth, pleasant experiences have become the norm for vast swaths of humans around the globe. So people, especially in the United States and especially in the middle class, now expect a continual series of pleasant events and are increasingly averse to unpleasant experiences of any kind, while many other folks around the world, even in so-called developed economies, are shelved, blocked, and otherwise excluded from these pleasures. Add to that the advertising-enhanced cultural message that, if you don't manage to line up the next pleasant experience, you're kind of a loser, and you start to see what a honey-tipped trap this all really is.

It's the second prong of consumerism, though, that concerns me most. At this level, we tend to harbor the sense that other people are not agents in their own right. Instead, they become, primarily at least, the sources of our pleasure. This kind of consumerism is like a blend of patriarchy and objectification on the rocks with a twist. We see it in nearly every arena of post-capitalist global society. And sexuality is no exception. Put simply, consuming people as objects means that everything we do is about either getting somebody or giving ourselves away. It undermines our dignity, from both sides. Boys are taught to look and take. Girls are taught to be looked at and to give. And nonbinary folks are often shoved to the margins, disqualified from playing a role in the whole giddy production.

The message here is that this combination of objectifying patriarchal consumerism leads to a strange shallowing, a disembodiment, a living at arm's length from oneself, as if you were always looking in, and not kindly, at your every move, your every body part. And more and more, these dynamics are meta-gendered, in that they impact men and women and those who don't identify in the binary, without particular discrimination, putting us all at risk for weirdly pervasive and unexamined suffering in the realm of sex, sexuality, and just about everything else.

Okay, so now we know the problem: objectifying patriarchal consumerism—or that dynamic, fluid, and complex set of processes by which

- men are first,
- perspective is outsourced, and
- everything, including other people, becomes a commodity.

So that's the problem with a whole lot of things in the post-modern, post-industrial age, but it's especially the problem with sexuality. Because when you apply these three shorthands to sexuality, you can see clearly how sex would be very much not good, right? I mean, how are we supposed to make sex good when men's pleasure is central and everyone else's pleasure is secondary? That's not good for men or for women, and it's certainly not good for those who don't fit easily into these rigidly scripted categories. How are we supposed to make sex good when we're being asked to continually stand outside of ourselves looking in with judge-y, evaluating eyes? And how are we supposed to make sex good—make it rich, make it wholesome and connected—when we're being trained, every moment of every day, to treat the world and all its people as nonsentient quasi-products to be consumed for our pleasure?

The answer is that when we treat ourselves and others in this way, when we live the mainstream, globalized, mechanized, capitalized ethos of our times, our sex will not be very good. It will not be very good at all.

So what's the answer? Four simple words: *take back your body*.

TAKE BACK YOUR BODY

In the beginning of this chapter I talked a little about that first moment of body shame. That moment when I put on my new turtleneck at ten years old, saw my belly, and suddenly and irrevocably divorced my body. I became, in that moment, a divided person, with one part of me living in the body while another part of me stood somehow at arm's length, in a continuous and horrified state of judgment, looking shamefully, angrily back at myself, wishing and willing it to be different.

By age fifteen, this bizarre twin consciousness, this sense of being two different selves, one torturing the other, had solidified to the point where I stood for long minutes in front of the mirror, staring at my mostly naked body every morning and every evening, looking for flaws. I began to exercise, then to over-exercise, then to control my eating, and then to over-control my eating. While I was lucky to never fully tip into anorexia, my eating—or lack of it—hit a painful crescendo during my two years in a sorority. I ate almost nothing, lost too much weight, and successfully landed the hottest boy on campus, a bronze-skinned Filipino American quarterback whom I accompanied (externally smiling, internally freaking out) through a rotating door of fraternity parties.

How was the sex? you might ask.

Not good. I mean, we loved each other. He tried his best. But by this point, internalized patriarchy was the daily weather pattern inside and I had no idea what I actually wanted. I didn't know what turned me on. Or if anything really turned me on. And all the cultural signposts seemed to point to making myself as ravishingly desirable as possible, without too much concern for what my body actually needed. And so most of our sex consisted of me turning him on and then going numb. Waiting until we were done so that I could go on a run or to the gym, or back to my dorm to tell my friends that we were, after all, having sex.

A sad state of affairs. And one that continued with my next boyfriend, a lovely human and wonderful friend who should have just stayed a friend but instead we ended up dating and then living together for four years after college. Sex? Same as before.

So what changed? Well, things started to change as my meditation practice gained traction in my midtwenties. And shifted again when I discovered yoga. Body-centered psychotherapy has also been a big, glorious, super-win. But the biggest shift—the seismic transformation—happened in the midst of a six-month meditation retreat all alone in a cabin in the mountains of southern Oregon. I had no phone, no computer, no electricity, no running water—and I had nothing to do but look at my own mind, feel my own heart, and know my own body, hour after hour after hour, day after day after day.

I wish I could say this long retreat was an entirely pleasant experience. I'd like to tell you I was filled with light, that angels danced, that I was elevated, blissful—and, in fact, those things do happen on meditation retreats (sometimes).

But not this time. This time, from just about the moment I first closed that cabin door behind me and the pickup truck that had dropped me off drove away down the long dirt road, I was struck by a clenching dread. That dread settled around me as I unpacked my things. It followed me to bed.

It was there when I woke up. And then for one hundred and eighty-something days it was my ever-present companion.

Were there thoughts that accompanied this dread? Indeed there were. All the same thoughts I always had. Except magnified. Amplified. Spinning me around and dragging me down. Shame thoughts. Guilt thoughts. Self-doubt, self-disgust, loneliness. The utter certainty that I wasn't good enough, not thin enough, not worthy enough. Oh, and the unrelenting hatred of my body. That particular variety of unfiltered self-loathing. Yep. That was me. Alone. In a cabin. For months.

I always tell people that it was during this stretch of time that I learned the true meaning of compassion. Firsthand. For myself and for everyone. Every morning waking up alone. Every evening sleeping alone. And nothing in between but knowing the body and watching the mind. Knowing breath, knowing the crunch of a sour apple, knowing the steps of my feet on crusty snow, the swirling thoughts of helplessness and despair. And just being with it. Remembering the meditation instructions again and again—just be with it. Just know. Awareness has room for everything.

And it did. It truly did. Awareness didn't let me down. By the end of that grueling, endless, lonesome retreat, I was a different human. And I felt, for the first time, that I could handle my whole life. Handle anything and everything. And that my body—this body, just as it is—was not only good enough: it was magic.

AND ANOTHER THING...

Let's Talk about Consent

Before we move on, let's take a quick minute here to talk about consent. Because when we're talking about having good sex–sex that aligns with our values and honors our own and our partner's body– we're always talking about consensual sex. Here's the thing: consent is not a confusing topic. Let me repeat that: consent is not a confusing topic. But here are a few simple guidelines for those of us who might still be figuring it out.[1]

1. Yes means yes.

   As a culture, for some reason we used to think that when somebody didn't explicitly say "no," that meant they wanted to have sex. That's a ridiculous standard. The true standard is that somebody tells you, really clearly and through words or obvious gestures, that they want to engage in sexual acts with you at this particular moment in time. If they're not doing/saying that, then you can assume they're not into it and you don't have consent.

2. It's moment to moment.

   One minute it could be yes, the next minute it could be no. This happens. And it's okay. Another thing that happens is that one partner can be into one level of sexual intimacy and not another or might like one position or sensation or encounter and not another. So if there's hesitation or objection or prevarication, consent has been revoked and some communication needs to happen before moving forward.

3. Enthusiastic consent is the goal.

   Which leads us to the gold standard: enthusiastic consent. Enthusiastic consent means both partners are really into what's happening and they are communicating this to each other with some degree of exuberance—through words, touch, expressions, and all the rest. Not only that, but they're checking in with each other as things progress. They're saying yes, taking it moment by moment, lighting a mutual fire. Anything less than enthusiastic consent is no consent at all.

Okay, glad we got that out of the way. Now let's jump back into how we're going to make this consensual sex really good.

HOW TO MAKE SEX GOOD

Most of us are never going to hole ourselves up in a cabin with no running water and no electricity and no cell reception for six months. And I'm not sure I even recommend it. I bought that little ticket to cabinland after doing a whole lot of training with a whole lot of very skilled meditation teachers. And I am also the recipient of many requisite privileges—race, class, nationality, and more—that even allowed me to consider such an option.

The good news, though, is that for the whole of humanity, who largely have no real interest in meditating alone ten hours a day for half a year, there are still ways to take back your body. What follows is not, I am sorry to say, a guide to really awesome sex, per se. (If you *are* looking for a guide to really awesome sex, the best book I have come across is *Urban Tantra* by Barbara Carrellas. Definitely pick that one up if you have a chance.) What I'll be offering here, instead, is a guide to taking back your body so that you can truly connect with your partner and find your own way into the good sex you've always wanted—or used to have and would like to get back. So here we go.

Unplug

Honestly, I can't believe it's taken us this long to drop in this all-important piece of contemporary semi-Buddhist advice. Come to think of it, we probably should have just started the book by recommending that you unplug. The entire book, in fact, could be called "unplug." But that ship has sailed and the book is mostly written and the publisher already has a title, so let me just say really quickly here:

This is maybe the most important thing we'll say in this entire book.

No big deal. But you might want to pay attention for a minute.

Everything I've been talking about thus far in this chapter, from objectifying patriarchal consumerism to my own little (ahem, big) journey of divorcing and then re-inhabiting my body, takes place in the context of the storming gale force of, yes, technology. Social media, in particular, which is, by its very nature, suffused with all the very messaging we've been unpacking here. If we want to make sex good, we need to take a break from all that.

For instance, let's say you have a lovely partner. Let's say you identify as a woman and she does, too. Let's say you're both in your early twenties, both graduated from college, both working full-time. Both tired, in other words. And let's say you live in a big city on the West Coast of the United States, just for kicks, and maybe you just moved in together, and what was a spontaneously flaming sex life just, almost overnight, sort of fizzled out. And now you're reading this book and looking for some good advice.

The first piece of good advice is to unplug. As in, when you both get home on a Wednesday night in winter after a rainy, raucous, exhausting commute, and you've just looked at each other and decided to order takeout and you both have the simultaneous impulse to pull out your Androids and start scrolling brainlessly through social media. Right then. That's when you hit airplane mode. On both your phones. And just kind of take each other in.

Slow Down

That's hard enough, isn't it? Because often, when we've had a long day in a long week in a long year of working and talking and traveling and shopping and spending and saving, the last thing we want to do is actually give our attention to another person. It's just too much.

But here's the thing: good sex doesn't happen without good attention. And since good, wholesome, fullhearted attention is *the* lost art of human consciousness in post-industrial societies, we're going to have to take deliberate steps to bring it back online.

Which means that, after you turn off your phones, I'd recommend making a concerted effort to slow down together. Think of it as a kind of foreplay. A thoroughly un-sexy foreplay, to be sure, sans lubes and vibrating rubber, but foreplay nonetheless. Because foreplay, as I see it, is about actually feeling yourself, your mind and your body, in this moment, free of the past, free of the future, free of distracting fantasies. And that's exactly what we're asking you to do when we're asking you to slow down.

One important point: slowing down does not necessarily mean talking. In fact, you might want to skip the whole "How was your day thing?" for now. (Those conversations are so much better after a few good orgasms, anyway, don't you think?) Instead, maybe just lie down on the floor together. Right on your back. Right on your rug. Side by side. Maybe don't even hold hands yet. Maybe just feel what it's like to be tired. Or doubtful. Or horny. The trick here is to get extremely sweet with yourself. Let a warm awareness begin to just know your experience, just like we talked about in the meditation chapter. And maybe repeat some of the kindness phrases that we talked about in the chapter on not being a jerk. Start with yourself. Start with just taking care of your own mind.

If you both like to meditate, try meditating a bit. Or if meditation isn't really your thing, just lie there and do nothing for a minute. Either way, the idea here is to let the mind and body start to unwind, relax, downshift.

Let Your Body Be the Guide

Once you've been lying around for a good, long while—maybe twenty minutes, maybe more—then it might be time to check in with your body. What does your body want right now? What would actually turn you on? Maybe a little music could be good. Or how about a bath together? Or, hell, maybe you're both ready to jump straight into leather and whips. That all depends on you. But see if you can find a way to make this a mutually guided exploratorium, a sensual reaching together in the unknown dark. I mean, not the literal dark. It's fine to have some lights on if you want. But the dark of the body, feeling into your body, and both your bodies, together, not quite sure yet what you'll find. Let these bodies lead you into what's next, whether it's something new and exciting or something routine and comforting. No judgment, just following what's next.

Of course, this is a relationship, right? So you'll need to navigate needs: overlapping needs, divergent needs, all kinds of needs and wants and messiness. You might need to pause and talk gently to each other. Or maybe this is one of those times where things just click and you get on the bullet train and go. You could let each time be a little different. And it will be a little different, if you really let your body be the guide.

Sex, like every relational human undertaking, has a kind of ethics, with its own guideposts, communions, pushes and pulls. When we come into the body, when we pay close attention to what we're feeling and to the feelings of another, we can naturally begin to discover this organic, uncharted code, this integrity of the heart. I don't mean to say it will be easy, and I certainly don't mean to suggest that sex should always be gentle or New Age-y, with deep breathing and lots of silk. If you like it rough, great, that can be really hot. If you're into multiple partners, play parties, polyamory, then hell, go for broke. But whatever you do, this staying with the body is a gateway to making sex good for you, and making sex good for others, which, of course, ties neatly into the innermost marrow of the Buddha's most foundational advice on our sexual selves: *don't misuse sexuality.*

Don't misuse it. Which is to say, don't cause harm, not

to yourself and not to others. And in fact, as we really start to tune in and understand the unacknowledged dialogues that our bodies are having, one with another, we might also begin to see how the messages from earlier chapters of this book are weaving their way in, quite naturally, to our forays into union and communion and carnal intimacy. We might see, for instance, how important it is to be clear with ourselves and our partners (chapter 6); why we'd want to say what's true, even when it's difficult (chapter 4); how much we actually want to give sensually and receive sensually (chapter 3); how sex can be a kind of healing and help (chapter 2); and how important returning to the body, in formal and informal meditation, really is (chapter 1). But all of this, really, grows out of sidestepping the tsunami of over-information, slowing down—way down—and letting the body be your guide.

A Little Meditation
TAKE BACK YOUR BODY

So let's experiment with the three steps I just ran through: unplug, slow down, and let your body be the guide. Take a short pause from your normal reading pace so you can move through this exercise more fully embodied.

First, take a minute to put your phone on airplane mode, close your laptop, and maybe move into your bedroom or a place that's relatively free of electronics and maybe even people and pets.

Now get in a comfortable position and slow down. You could pause here, put a hand on your heart and a hand on your belly, stop reading, and simply breathe. Feel your body and your breath. Allow all the thoughts to slow down, unwind, loosen, and release.

And now, let your body do the practice. Simply feel your bodily sensations, from your head down to your feet. If you want, you can do a simple body scan, moving your attention down your body like a wave washing through you. And then when you're done, fill your body with awareness like you'd fill a cup with water. Feel every cell full of bright clear awareness.

Rest here for a while.

That's it. You can bring this kind of attention with you, wherever you go, and especially while you are getting down with your partner. Guaranteed, you will have a better time when you are fully in your body like this. In fact, you might think about coming back to this exercise before sex for the next couple weeks, or even for a couple months, just to get in the habit of being in your body before, during, and after sex.

AND ANOTHER THING...

P.S.: We Also Hold Trauma in Our Bodies

It's all well and good to ask you to fully inhabit your body. And of course, sex *will* be better when you reside within the warm knowing of this sensual frame. But let's not forget: we hold trauma in our bodies. Often in our most private places and parts. While this is likely more true for some of us than others, to some extent, it's true for us all. So as you're beginning to take your body back—as you unplug, and slow down, and let yourself be guided— remember to take care and tread lightly.

What does that mean? To tread lightly means to go slow. It means to back off a bit if you hit tension, pain, emotional ripples, or other warning signs. The message of this chapter is to honor your body, to live in the experience of *what's really happening now*. And so if what's really happening now is that you're starting to panic, or you're having flashbacks, or something just doesn't feel right for you, remember that you're allowed to ease up, take a break, and proceed at your own pace. Your partner will understand. Or if your partner doesn't understand, then it may be time for a big sit-down kind of conversation.

At any rate, if you're doing some of the exercises from this book—whether in this sex chapter or in any chapter—and you start to hit a trauma response (heart racing, sweating, flashbacks, irritability, a weird sort of detachment), there are four simple steps you can follow to help ground yourself.[2]

- *Don't push yourself.* When you've touched into trauma, go slowly. Gently explore the edge of your sensations, with a balanced and caring attention. Don't just push through—give yourself a lot of breaks to rest, and then go back to exploring the edges with a lot of mindfulness and care.
- *Look around.* Let your eyes wander about the room or whatever environment you're in. See color, shape, texture. Just notice that you are seeing stuff, and notice that you are in a safe space. This pause to take in your surroundings allows the nervous system to relax and orient to the present moment— so that you can let go of the anxiety or trigger or whatever is happening.
- *Toggle.* Go back and forth between sensing into your body and then looking around and taking a break. Don't dig too deeply or too quickly. Trust the body's ability to release trauma slowly, but don't force things.
- *Get support.* Talking to someone about this can be really helpful. Especially a trained professional who specializes in trauma work. You can also check out our resources section for stuff that we recommend.

NO SEX IS GREAT SEX

Just a final word before we close out this chapter on making sex good. And this is a special lesson that took years and years for me to learn: *No sex can be great sex.*

What the heck does that mean? To start with, it means that, if you're on the asexuality spectrum—as many people are—and you don't really have a big yen for skin-on-skin action, that's perfectly fine. That's great, even. Don't believe the mass media hype, this constant messaging that sexual satisfaction is the only satisfaction, that excitement is the pinnacle of existence.

Sometimes you just want a good cup of tea.

And don't underestimate the power of your aliveness. For me, accepting that I don't always love or want or need sex has been supremely liberating. It's not some kind of handicap or problem, like our culture wants us to believe. Some days I'm a sexual person. Other days I'm not. Some days I want to get it on. Other days I don't. And that's okay. It took me years to learn to just be okay with following the natural rhythms of my body, and of my partner's body, and letting them guide me with gentleness and honesty.

What I've noticed, at least for myself, is that I am an erotic person. An embodied human. I love the world. I love sensation. But that doesn't always have to be sex for me. It could be running in the morning with the slanting light and birdsong and warm air. Or singing really loud in the shower. Being alive and fully in your body is very erotic, and holding a pose in yoga can be just as good as getting racy in bed. Don't let the culture tell you there's something wrong with you if you take pleasure in things other than sex. Do your thing and be proud.

No sex is great sex can also mean that, if you're not having sex with a friend or lover right now, there's plenty of sex you can have on your own. Especially if you're a woman, and you've received messages about the wrongs of masturbation, I'd encourage you to get down with your bad self and start exploring your labia. It's fun and it makes sex with a partner about twelve times better when that person comes along.

And, finally, through meditation, you can learn to ride waves of sexuality, even when you're not having sex. Sexual energy is just energy. So treat it that way. Treat it like any other sense impression. Use your meditation. Feel it deeply, let it pass through you, let it energize you, and then put that energy into whatever wonderful world-saving moment you're living in. Since you're not defined by sex, and especially since you're hip to the globalized exploitation of objectified images and internet advertising, you don't necessarily need to follow every sexual fantasy to its foregone conclusion. I have found that this ability to direct sexual energy instead of letting it direct me can be a game changer.

A LAST CHECK-IN

Let's finish where we started, with some contemplation about sex. And, just to end with a familiar frame, let's revisit those questions we asked at the beginning of the chapter. Get cozy. Feel your body. And then ask,

- What is sex about, for me?
- What is my version of good, powerful, meaningful sex?
- How do my deepest values inform my sex life?
- How does my sex life express my deepest values?

Finally, what's one thing—one small, doable thing—you can do today that will move you in the direction of the sex (or non-sex) that you really, truly want? Maybe it's buying a really great cup of cocoa. Or going skiing. Or getting naked with yourself. Or listening to your favorite song. Or buying a ukulele. Or writing a love letter.

Wonderful. Now go out and do that one thing.

Just about all of us, I think, are entangled, in one way or another, to one extent or another, in the trinity of bad sex. *Objectifying patriarchal consumerism* is running us around, grinding us down, and drying up our life-affirming orgasmic potential. But never fear, you can *take back your body*. And how will you take back your living, breathing, surprising, and wonderful body? With three simple steps: *unplug, slow down*, and *let your body be the guide*.

Oh, and also, don't be fooled. It's totally fine to not want sex every day of your life.

Next stop: clarity. Because remember that moment we talked about way back in the beginning of the book, where the young Prince Siddhartha stood strong in his values, put his hand on the earth, and said "No, thanks" to the demon Mara, thereby attaining a kind of final steadiness right in the middle of the storm? That clarity was not just something the Buddha accomplished in one single moment; it was something he cultivated, step by step, every moment along the way to that final moment. Likewise, we can all set ourselves on a similar (though certainly not identical) path of daily clearing stuff up as we learn to ride the waves and weirdness of our particular storms.

STAY CLEAR
Craig

The final piece of advice the Buddha has to offer on how to feel valuable and whole and happy while the whole wide world burns is simple: don't get drunk.

Whoops. I just felt a disturbance in the force: hundreds—no thousands—of readers around the world putting this book down and picking up their iPhone.

Well, just to keep things interesting, and since I've never been one to back down from a bad argument, I'll throw in another one:

Don't get high, either.

Don't shoot heroin, don't smoke crack, don't crush pills up into itty-bitty piles of blue powder and then blow them up your nasal passage for that lovely little head rush of self-dissolving bliss you've been waiting for since Thursday morning. Also don't smoke weed and don't sniff glue and don't take your dad's prescriptions and don't drink entire bottles of cough syrup and watch your face melt in the bathroom mirror.

Don't do any of these things. Or the Buddha will be mad at you.

Just kidding. Well, not about steering clear of substances that cloud the mind, gunk up your judgment, and generally make you less able to adequately live the life you most want to live right now. Not kidding about that part. Just the Buddha being mad part. He won't be mad. He died years ago, after all.

So what's the deal? And what's it got to do with staying grounded right in the middle of the tornado-like maelstrom of information, culture wars, technology, politics, overwork, underpay, and your neighbors who won't turn the music down at 3 a.m.?

Well, maybe it will be helpful to talk a bit about my own process with all this.

YEARS OF LIVING HAZILY

I hail from a family of alcoholics. All three of my parents (dad, mom, stepmom) drank heavily when I was young. All three of them were sincerely and thoroughly invested in what I think of as the "mystique of intoxication"—this backward, highly branded, advertising-infused assumption that getting sloshed is somehow part of the good life, that it's sophisticated even, and that it brings people together.

I therefore grew up simultaneously horrified by their behavior—screaming matches, drunk car accidents, extremely poor financial decisions—and yet also somehow sold on the underlying premise that getting drunk was pretty cool. I associated alcohol with being relaxed, with sex, with good times, and with lavishly talking to people at parties that, looking back, I never really wanted to be at in the first place.

I'm astonished and a little dismayed to report that this sort of beleaguered thinking lasted a very, very long time for me. Even after many small and big lessons on why alcohol is not such an obvious winner, I continued to drink to ease social anxiety, take the edge off at the end of a long day, and, more to the point, just because it was somehow inexplicably a part of who I was—an indispensable allocation of my cultural heritage.

Until it wasn't. Because very gradually—and this process took years—as I saw that getting drunk led to more regrets than fond memories, I stopped getting really truly toasted. And then, very slowly, something fundamental shifted. I started to notice that the kind of relaxation that alcohol provides is, in essence, a sort of dullness. As I gradually fell in love with the clarity of mind that comes from meditation and mindfulness, I slowly cut down on those moments when drinking alcohol seemed like a thrilling proposition.

Finally, I was just down to drinking on special occasions and at fancy restaurants when one day I realized, sort of all of a sudden, that alcohol and celebration were not, in fact, one and the same thing, and that I could celebrate the heck out of something or someone without getting a little tipsy. So I pretty much stopped.

These days I barely drink at all. I mean, if I'm at someone's house and they're drinking wine, I'll have a glass with dinner. On a wild night, I might even have two. But I rarely drink at home and I can't remember the last time I got drunk. Unsurprisingly, my life feels no less sophisticated, my connections with others have only improved, and when I say or do stupid things, I have no one to blame but my own bad mental habits.

Still, there will be a loss. Whenever we give up one socially sanctioned behavior for another perhaps-less-socially-sanctioned behavior, there is a loss. Some friends will not cheer you on; some friends will, in fact, keep drunkenly handing you Long Island ice teas until you awkwardly decide to leave the party. And yet. Other friends will appear in their place. And you will have the presence of mind to know them to be good friends worth hanging out with. Or good friends worth having sex with. Or good friends worth marrying.

Okay, yes, good story. But what does all this actually have to do with staying steady in the midst of everything?

THREE GOOD REASONS TO STAY CLEAR

Staying clear is the last important guideline the Buddha offers. It's a bit different from recommending that we don't kill or steal or lie or misuse our libido. But still, it has important implications. Let me break it down for you. If you don't get drunk, the following things will happen:

1. You'll make fewer dumb mistakes.
2. You'll have more clear moments.
3. You might be surprised.

If you quit drinking alcohol *you'll make fewer dumb mistakes.* This is just a simple fact of life. You won't lose your phone because you're drunk, or pick up a three-hundred-dollar bar tab because you're drunk, or have to deal with your heartbreak and self-disgust after getting drunk and sleeping with your ex whom you can't seem to stop texting on Friday nights when you get home a little sloshed and can't remember how bad you felt last time you did this. Then there are the affairs that happen when you're drunk, or high, or blasted on cocaine. And the DUIs. Or just the hurtful things you say to your partner or friend or sibling that you wouldn't say if you were calm and focused and not three-and-a-half drinks into an otherwise pleasant celebration of their birthday.

So you'll make fewer dumb mistakes. And dumb mistakes, it turns out, account for a whole lot of the energy that we throw away on the spinning orb of crazy we call our lives. Really, truly, when you stop making dumb mistakes—verbal mistakes, sex mistakes, spending mistakes, other mistakes—you'll notice how much more vitality you have for what's important to you. Like making a positive contribution to the people around you whenever you can.

You'll also have more clear moments if you stop drinking alcohol and getting high. One clear moment leads to another clear moment. Which leads to another clear moment, and that kind of momentum grows on itself. When you then begin to build in some of what we've talked about over the past hundred or so pages, those clear moments mixed with kindness and generosity and actual good sex and all the rest will start to lead to real, genuine, salt-of-the-earth sanity. And when most of your moments start to feel pretty clear, and pretty good to you, it doesn't matter quite as much what other people think or say or do.

Which is not to say you won't be engaged. Be engaged! We need you engaged. Do your thing. Go to work. Fight for justice and equity, fight for love and people getting health care and education and good green forests and, god help us all, significant carbon reductions. Stand up for what you believe in. Meet people who are different from you. Ask how you can help, and then do that thing. Also, rest. Take care of yourself. Get enough water and vegetables and good, deep sleep. Do all of this clearly, with purpose, with your goals in the front of your mind.

Finally, I'll just say, *you might be surprised.* I was surprised, frankly, to see how much I didn't need alcohol and drugs in my life. I can remember the times when I did. I can remember the heights of anxiety I experienced at parties, graduations, performances, or just sitting on my living room couch. I remember what it was like to have blood pumping a bit too fast through my veins, the very real sense that I should flee, and I remember drinking or just taking a puff or two of a little something to clear those moments.

But as I progressed on the path of meditation and began to see its benefits and, especially, as I began to right the ship of my life through looking at these ethical checkpoints we've been talking about, more and more I just didn't need to cloud my mind with some external ethanol. The simple act of living and breathing, along with clearer and clearer intentions around what I'm living for, became enough. More than enough. It's become a delight.

Now, you could respond to all this, "Thank you very much, you make some interesting points, but the fact is I really like to get drunk with my friends."

Great! Wonderful, I would say back to you, then go get drunk with your friends. Do all the things you love. Do them fully. And then just step back and notice. Let that mindfulness muscle you've been building stay alert at the back of your mind—notice what's happening as you reach for the water pipe, or notice what's happening after that third drink. Notice, too, what it's like to wake up in the morning. Track your thoughts. Track your feelings. How are you feeling in your body at 10 a.m.? The name of the game here in these semi-Buddhist suggestions for staying steady and living sweet is to *notice and then notice and then notice* some more—and eventually your mind will begin to incline toward what serves you best.

For you, maybe that will be drinking Friday nights, smoking an occasional joint, and tripping on acid a couple times a year. Or maybe that will be this year. And then next year it will be a bit less alcohol and a smidgeon more cannabis.

Who knows? We certainly don't. But we have all the confidence that you can find out for yourself.

AND ANOTHER THING...
What About Hallucinogens?

Let me say first off: I am so not an expert on the topic of hallucinogens. I've tried them a few times. I've read about them some. Many of our most beloved meditation teachers had profound early awakening experiences while doing acid or mushrooms or peyote or whatever. That said, I'm not here to advocate for the use of entheogens on the path of spiritual awakening. And I'm not here to talk them down, either. What I can say is the right dose at the right time for the right person with the right guidance might really open you up. Or, the wrong dose at the wrong time for the wrong person . . . well, that can get very unpleasant.

At any rate, let's see what the research has to say.

On the positive side, probably the most convincing science has come out of Johns Hopkins University, where Dr. Roland Griffiths and a team of medical researchers put a small sample of cancer patients through a carefully controlled series of psilocybin trips.[1] What they found is pretty convincing. For about 80 percent of these cancer patients, tripping on mushrooms (or at least the chemical compound derived from mushrooms) was a life-changing experience. It made them less depressed, less anxious, increased their quality of life, increased their sense of meaning in life, made them more optimistic, and helped them with death anxiety. Even more impressive, these self-report ratings were not only confirmed by third-party raters in the lab. They were corroborated by family members and friends at home. Plus, the results held up six months after. So that's cool.

Other studies, though perhaps less well designed, have established positive effects from the careful and controlled use of LSD, ayahuasca, peyote, and MDMA (ecstasy). But the real truth of the matter is that, since the US government has hated on hallucinogens for so darn long, we have only a scant research base on which to sing the praises of these very powerful chemical compounds. The most we can say, at this point, from a scientific perspective is, *Well, this looks interesting.*

Now to the dark side. Early studies, mostly on LSD, claimed that acid and other similar drugs were a cause of first-break psychosis. Since LSD was illegal, though, there were few opportunities to verify these early reports, which were often based on records kept in emergency rooms rather than from well-controlled drug trials. Still, for years medical schools have used these studies to teach their students about the risks of LSD. Now that things have been loosening up legally, however, two[2] epidemiological studies[3] have shown no links between hallucinogens and psychosis—or any other mental health problems. So it's possible that LSD, peyote, and all these other drugs are not as dangerous as we once thought.

Still, people do have bad trips. If you're going to try a mind-exploding entheogen like peyote or LSD, please make sure you're careful. Surround yourself with good friends. Get a reliable guide who can take care of you. Find a safe place. And have a darn good reason—a crystal clear intention—for what you're trying to get from this (very intense) experience.

STAY CLEAR

Okay, now that we've talked about what not to do (alcohol, most drugs) and we've talked about what to maybe sometimes sort of do if you're really careful (hallucinogens), what might be helpful to actually go ahead and unequivocally do?

Actually, there's a lot we'd recommend you try to do, but all of these suggestions, really this entire book, fall neatly into just two words: *stay clear.*

Stay clear. Moment by moment, hour by hour, day by day, first today, then tomorrow, stay clear. Keep a clear mind. Keep a clear heart. Even in the face of everything falling down around you. Simply stay clear.

Tall order? Maybe. It's not easy. But it's possible. Or usually possible. And even if staying clear is only *sometimes* possible, it's certainly worthwhile.

So what do we mean by staying clear? We mean *remember chapters 1 through 5 of this very book.* We mean that when somebody gets all up in your business, and you want to destroy them—verbally, online, or with a cream pie in their face—you step back for a moment. You take a breath. You remember some of the suggestions that these two friendly Buddhists, Devon and Craig, blathered on about. And instead of destroying said person who's getting all up in your business, you find another way. Best-case scenario, you even look for a way to be helpful.

Or maybe you're living in a world of mental scarcity, when you think nothing is enough for you, and you're shot through with every desire known to humans. You're having a rough day, feeling lonely, and you think to yourself, *If I just had that other boy's boyfriend, then everything would be all right.* And you pause for a minute, remember the Buddha's recommendation to not take what's not freely offered (even boyfriends), and then put all that wanting energy into something at least slightly more productive and life affirming. You'll feel better, more resourced, in the long run. Maybe not right this moment. But over time, as you start to get the hang of all this.

Or let's say you find yourself right in the middle of telling a fabulous lie. And then clarity sets in. And, fabulously, you walk your way out of that lie and find a way to say what's true. Or at the end of the day you find yourself being all grabby and selfish with sex, but then you recognize a better road, and you take that road, and you make sex good.

Or maybe you've just had your 99th moment of the day when you want to check out and binge-watch Netflix, or scroll mindlessly through social media, or eat the thing that won't actually make you feel better, or read the news story that will do nothing to edify you but everything to flip you out—and at that very 99th moment you remember what you really want in life and then apply that deeper desire to this trivial-seeming instance, and decide instead to do a kindness meditation, or text a sweet little something to a friend, or just go for a walk around the block.

You get the picture. Each theme we've talked about here, each ethical guidepost, requires clarity, presence of mind, commitment. It's awfully hard to live in these states when you're zonked on oxycodone all the time. It's actually not completely easy to live in these states even without the use or abuse of mind-altering substances.

So how do we live with clarity?

SECLUSION

We live in a world that never shuts off. You might have grown up in this world. You might take this world for granted. But it's important to recognize that this is the first time in the entire run of human history that such a world has ever even come close to existing. Ever. As in, there has never been a time, anywhere, anytime, when there were literally thousands—no, millions—of gigabytes of entertainment available to your bubbling neurons at any time of day, any time of night, any moment, without exception, at the swipe of a finger or the click of a button.

The 1,001 TV channels, the movie studios, the game makers, the social media gods, the online shopping emperors, the newscasters, the talk radio hosts, the podcasters, the YouTubers, and anyone else trying to grab your attention (and your cash) for a split second of your busily overloaded day would like you to think that this overload is a good thing. They would like you to think that you live in the best of all possible realms, where your every need will be met by the continually expanding galaxy of products, products, products, and that you will live a happier, more informed, more gracious life if you just tune in to . . . whatever they happen to be selling.

There's only one problem. It's nonsense.

Worse than nonsense. In our humble semi-Buddhist opinion, it's one of the biggest lies our post-industrial civilization has ever been sold.

Because as we all know by now, people in the United States and the rest of the hyper-informational world are no happier than they used to be. Having everything-and-more at your fingertips every moment of every day and night doesn't actually bump your well-being up a notch. If anything, it bogs you down.

So are we recommending that you walk away from it all and join a monastery? Actually, that would be a great idea! Monasteries are some of the few remaining pockets of balance in an otherwise maddening world.

But, no, we're not suggesting *everybody* reading this book join a monastery. What we're suggesting, instead, is that everyone reading this book bring a bit of the monastery into their life. Because what a monastery provides, at its most elementary level, is seclusion.

Now *seclusion* isn't the most popular word these days. Nobody on the morning talk shows raves about their practice of seclusion. Quite the opposite. But from a Buddhist perspective—and this is our perspective—seclusion is an absolutely essential ingredient to any sane life, especially if you're living in an urbanized, post-industrial, information-heavy dreamscape.

Seclusion itself, though, can look like a lot of different things. One seclusion practice we like a lot is just turning everything off (you know, like we talked about in the last chapter). Powering down the computers. Turning off the phones. And just being. Sure, you'll probably fall asleep. But that's great! Because most of us are really, really exhausted.

Then there's meditation. The ultimate seclusion practice. Take five minutes. Take ten minutes. Take half an hour. And just feel the breath. Feel the breath as it comes into the body. Feel the breath as it leaves the body. Every time a thought comes up, acknowledge that thought with an extra-generous helping of warmth and sweetness, and then go back to feeling the breath.

If meditation is tough for you—and it was tough for us at first, for sure—then use one of the five or six really, really good meditation apps out there.

Another revolutionary act of seclusion is taking a walk in the woods. Or a walk on the beach. Or a walk in the park. Just meandering, with nowhere to go and nothing to do, for half an hour, or an hour, or a whole day. Without your phone. Try it sometime. You might find that your mind rebels, but if you stick with the practice and let the mind spin a while, eventually it will settle, and you'll often find a new experience altogether: calm.

A Little Meditation
ONE BREATH

Here's one of our favorite mini seclusion exercises. Why? Because you can do it anywhere, anytime. We do this one in trains, planes, automobiles. We do it when we're feeling overwhelmed or stressed. We do it before big meetings and after little conversations. We do it multiple times a day.

Ready? Okay.

Close your eyes. (Or don't.) Take a big inhale, noticing all your sensations. Pay attention. Pause.

Then exhale, noticing all your sensations. Pay attention. Pause.

And that's it. Then go back to your day.

Or you can do this with three breaths:

Get ready.

Pay attention.

Breathe deep into your lungs, deep into your belly. And then exhale out, nice and slow. Two more times:

Inhale. Pause. Exhale. Pause.

Inhale. Pause. Exhale. Pause.

And then go back to your day.

So if you're not going to join a monastery, you can find ways to bring the monastery into your life. Find small moments of seclusion. Calm and clarity will gradually become part of these random moments. For me, since I work as a therapist, it means taking two minutes before my next client comes in, and just breathing in my office chair with my eyes closed. You can do these things. You really can. You can build these little moments of seclusion, these little resets, into your life.

So don't get drunk. Or high. Or if you *do* get drunk and/or high, track your experience, do some phenomenological accounting, and see for yourself when moderated intemperance serves you and when it doesn't. After all, teetotaling has some benefits. Like the fact that you'll make fewer dumb mistakes, have more clear moments, and you might even be surprised by how little you need to alter your consciousness with chemical compounds. Building on that, we suggest you set an intention in your life to *stay clear*. And we mean that in all the most obvious and not-so-obvious ways. Still, staying clear, in our experience, requires frequent mini-forays into intentional *seclusion*, and we've come to see these abbreviated quasi-retreats as not only essential to maintaining a modicum of clarity but also as one indispensable ingredient in an ever-developing strategy for surviving modern life.

SOME FINAL THOUGHTS

Friends! We are fast approaching the conclusion of our semi-Buddhist survival guide. It's been a wicked ride—fun, a little harrowing, certainly a very new experience for the two of us. We are grateful and honored you've come this far. Happy to have spent some time together.

Along the way we really loved telling you about how meditation might nudge your days into less stress, more focus, and a sweeter humanity. We hope you enjoyed reading about how to be less of a jerk and more of an amicable altruist. Also, that part where we waxed poetic about the wonders of generosity? That made at least *some* sense, right? Oh, and truth. And sex. Truth definitely seems important, and sex is also far from a trifling topic, what with being foundational to biology, emotions, relationships, society, and our general happiness on this planet. So it was cool we got to hang out with those two for a few pages.

Last but not least, though: clarity. We love clarity. In fact, maybe staying clear is the heartwood of the proverbial tree. The quintessence. The bottom line. Brass tacks, and all the rest. Because when we stay clear, really clear, about who we are, what we're about, and what we genuinely, truly want out of life, there is a lot less that can shake us up and make us crumble. Just look at the greats, if you need some inspiration. The Dalai Lama lost his entire country to an invading military force, yet he manages to be an ambassador of compassion and steadiness in the face of it all. Thich Nhat Hanh refused to take sides in the Vietnam War because of these very principles we've been unpacking along the way here. And even though it got to the point where his own government wanted him dead, he was able to stay clear and calm and kind, and he has never swerved from that path. Then there's Angela Davis, Desmond Tutu, Audre Lorde, Martin Luther King Jr., Greta Thunberg, St. Francis of Assisi, Dorothy Day, bell hooks, Matthieu Ricard, Roshi Joan Halifax, Mingyur Rinpoche, and a thousand other real-world sages, some historical and some living right now, who embodied and embody the principles of this book in real time with clarity and commitment and grace.

But here's the thing. The big take-home. The spectacular reveal. The Message with a capital M: *You, too, can do this.* It's not just for fancy historical figures or people who write books and give TED talks and share wisdom from the mountaintops. You really can stay clear, say what's true, give a little, make sex good, meditate occasionally, and be less of a jerk and more of a stable loving presence in your world. Right in the middle of everything. Even when the shit is hitting the fan, your housemate is on drugs, your job is a mess, your romance is shaky, and you don't know just exactly what you want to do with your life. Right there, in the middle of it all, you can find a little seclusion, perhaps do a little meditation, and reset your compass. *Okay,* you might say to yourself, as the two of us often do, *I don't know precisely exactly what to do. But I know who I am. I know what matters to me. And what matters to me is kindness, compassion, real friendship, doing good for others, contributing, taking care of myself, taking care of everyone I meet, and deeply knowing my experience in each moment of every day.*

Life, lived like that, becomes very immediate, very rich, and a whole lot more workable. So let the storms rage. Let the waves crash. Let the winds shriek and the demons sing. Because right at the center of the blizzard of stimulation that is modern life, and even with all your confusions and imperfections and sneaky little doubts, you can still place your hand on whatever patch of ground you're sitting on and say, *Today, in this moment anyway, I will be a slightly less dysregulated hot mess, a semi-still point in the spin, a builder of kindness and a bastion of decency. Or maybe I'll just shoot somebody a flyby smile and call it good.*

Cash, James Baraz, the Tergar instructors, Khenpo Tsultrim Gyamtso Rinpoche, Lama Karma Rinchen, and many more.

There are also so many dharma friends we'd love to thank. Friends whose conversation, ideas, feedback, and life examples have contributed in so many ways, subtle and not-so-subtle, to this book becoming this book. Too many to name here. But just to throw a few out into the world: Cortland Dahl, Kasumi Kato, Leandro Chernicoff, Daniela Labra, Richard Davidson (okay, Richie is more like a mentor), John and Anna Dunne, James Meadows, Annie Taylor, Christian Dillo, Gary Hardin, Scott Tusa, Alexis Santos, trudy mitchell-gilkey, La Sarmiento, Ann Gleig, Dan Harris, Lizzy Hoke, Celine Peccatte, Laura Kaiser, Evan Henritze, all the students in our psychology of mindfulness class at UW–Madison, the IMS Teacher Training Cohort (2018–2021), Community Dharma Leaders (4th edition; 2010–2012), everybody at the UW–Health MBSR Teacher Sangha, Rhonda Magee, Brooke Dodson-Lavelle, everybody at Madison Insight, everybody at Tergar Madison and Tergar International, everybody at Boulder Zen Center and Crestone Mountain Zen Center, not to mention KSC, KCC, KTL, All Sentient Beings, and anybody we just forgot but didn't mean to forget. Thanks for walking said meandering, knobby, sometimes perplexing, usually inspiring dharma path with us while offering advice, encouragement, support, curiosity, and just generally really good conversation.

Then there are all the wonderful humans who contributed very directly to this book. Matthew Zepelin, who one fine spring day asked us to submit a proposal to Shambhala Publications. Jennifer Brown, editor extraordinaire, who somehow found it in her heart to be our ally and cheerleader for this project, right from the early phases of pushing the book through the green-lighting process, all the way into the multiple drafts and edits and every other conceivable twist and turn. Katelin Ross, Tori Henson, Adria Batt, and KJ Grow, who got the word out. The incredible humans at I Ola Lāhui, who so wholeheartedly encouraged and sustained us through writing this darn thing. And, of course, our readers: Devin Berry, Rachel Flichtbeil, Matthew Hirschberg, Simon Goldberg, Gabrielle Farquhar, Rae Houseman and the ever-intrepid Susa Talan, who read multiple drafts and offered more of her time and energy and effort than seems reasonable. Thank you!

NOTES

Introduction

1. U. A. Tejaniya, *Awareness Alone Is Not Enough* (Selangor, Malaysia: Auspicious Affinity Press, 2008).

Chapter 1: Meditate

1. M. Szalavitz, "Q&A: Jon Kabat-Zinn Talks About Bringing Mindfulness Meditation to Medicine," *Time*, January 11, 2012, http://healthland.time.com/2012/01/11/mind-reading-jon-kabat-zinn-talks-about-bringing-mindfulness-meditation-to-medicine.

2. P. R. Goldin and J. J. Gross, "Effects of Mindfulness-Based Stress Reduction (MBSR) on Emotion Regulation in Social Anxiety Disorder," *Emotion* 10, no. 1 (2010): 83.

3. D. Goleman and R. J. Davidson, *Altered Traits: Science Reveals How Meditation Changes Your Mind, Brain, and Body* (New York: Penguin, 2017). This list is drawn almost word for word from *Altered Traits*, a book we highly recommend.

4. A. P. Jha, J. Krompinger, and M. J. Baime, "Mindfulness Training Modifies Subsystems of Attention," *Cognitive, Affective, and Behavioral Neuroscience* 7, no 2 (2007): 109–119.

5. H. G. Jo, S. Schmidt, E. Inacker, M. Markowiak, and T. Hinterberger, "Meditation and Attention: A Controlled Study on Long-Term Meditators in Behavioral Performance and Event-Related Potentials of Attentional Control," *International Journal of Psychophysiology* 99 (2016): 33–39.

6. A. Lutz, H. A. Slagter, N. B. Rawlings, A. D. Francis, L. L. Greischar, and R. J. Davidson, "Mental Training Enhances Attentional Stability: Neural and Behavioral Evidence," *Journal of Neuroscience* 29, no. 42 (2009): 13418–13427.

7. B. Schöne, T. Gruber, S. Graetz, M. Bernhof, and P. Malinowski, "Mindful Breath Awareness Meditation Facilitates Efficiency Gains in Brain Networks: A Steady-State Visually Evoked Potentials Study," *Scientific Reports* 8, no. 1 (2018): 13687.

8. M. Xu, C. Purdon, P. Seli, and D. Smilek, "Mindfulness and Mind Wandering: The Protective Effects of Brief Meditation in Anxious Individuals," *Consciousness and Cognition* 51, (2017): 157–165.

9. M. D. Mrazek, M. S. Franklin, D. T. Phillips, B. Baird, and J. W. Schooler, "Mindfulness Training Improves Working Memory Capacity and GRE Performance While Reducing Mind Wandering." *Psychological Science* 24, no. 5 (2013): 776–781.

10. H. Y. Weng, A. S. Fox, A. J. Shackman, D. E. Stodola, J. Z. Caldwell, M. C. Olson, G. M. Rogers, and R. J. David-

son, "Compassion Training Alters Altruism and Neural Responses to Suffering," *Psychological Science* 24, no. 7 (2013): 1171–1180.

11. Y. Kang, J. R. Gray, and J. F. Dovidio, "The Nondiscriminating Heart: Lovingkindness Meditation Training Decreases Implicit Intergroup Bias," *Journal of Experimental Psychology: General* 143, no. 3 (2014): 1306.

12. C. A. Hutcherson, E. M. Seppala, and J. J. Gross, "Loving-Kindness Meditation Increases Social Connectedness," *Emotion* 8, no. 5 (2008): 720–724.

13. P. Condon, G. Desbordes, W. B. Miller, and D. DeSteno, "Meditation Increases Compassionate Responses to Suffering," *Psychological Science* 24, no. 10 (2013): 2125–2127.

14. S. Parks, M. D. Birtel, and R. J. Crisp, "Evidence That a Brief Meditation Exercise Can Reduce Prejudice Toward Homeless People," *Social Psychology* 45 (2014): 458–465.

15. A. Lueke and B. Gibson, "Mindfulness Meditation Reduces Implicit Age and Race Bias: The Role of Reduced Automaticity of Responding," *Social Psychological and Personality Science* 6, no. 3 (2015): 284–291.

Chapter 2: Don't Be a Jerk

1. R. S. Edelstein, I. S. Yim, and J. A. Quas, "Narcissism Predicts Heightened Cortisol Reactivity to a Psychosocial Stressor in Men," *Journal of Research in Personality* 44, no. 5 (2010): 565–572.

2. J. T. Cheng, J. L. Tracy, and G. E. Miller, "Are Narcissists Hardy or Vulnerable? The Role of Narcissism in the Production of Stress-Related Biomarkers in Response to Emotional Distress," *Emotion* 13, no. 6 (2013): 1004.

3. F. Rhodewalt and C. C. Morf, "On Self-Aggrandizement and Anger: A Temporal Analysis of Narcissism and Affective Reactions to Success and Failure," *Journal of Personality and Social Psychology* 74, no. 3 (1998): 672.

4. J. D. Miller, W. K. Campbell, D. L. Young, C. E. Lakey, D. E. Reidy, A. Zeichner, and A. S. Goodie, "Examining the Relations Among Narcissism, Impulsivity, and Self-Defeating Behaviors," *Journal of Personality and Social Psychology* 77, no. 3 (2009): 761–794.

5. Dalai Lama. *Ethics for the New Millennium* (New York: Penguin, 2001).

6. C. A. Hutcherson, E. M. Seppala, and J. J. Gross, "Loving-Kindness Meditation Increases Social Connectedness," *Emotion* 8, no. 5 (2008): 720.

7. B. L. Fredrickson, M. A. Cohn, K. A. Coffey, J. Pek, and S. M. Finkel, "Open Hearts Build Lives: Positive Emotions, Induced Through Loving-Kindness Meditation, Build Consequential Personal Resources," *Journal of Personality and Social Psychology* 95, no. 5 (2008): 1045.

8. For a list of Tomasello's publications, see https://sites.duke.edu/tomasellolabduke/publications/.

9. M. Tomasello and A. Vaish, "Origins of Human Cooperation and Morality," *Annual Review of Psychology* 64 (2013): 231–255.

Chapter 3: Give a Little

1. W. M. Brown, N. S. Consedine, and C. Magai, "Altruism Relates to Health in an Ethnically Diverse Sample of Older Adults," *Journals of Gerontology Series B: Psychological Sciences and Social Sciences*, 60, no. 3 (2005): P143–P152.

2. M. J. Poulin, S. L. Brown, A. J. Dillard, and D. M. Smith, "Giving to Others and the Association Between Stress and Mortality," *American Journal of Public Health* 103, no. 9 (2013): 1649–1655.

3. T. K. Inagaki and N. I. Eisenberger, "Neural Correlates of Giving Support to a Loved One," *Psychosomatic Medicine* 74, no. 1 (2012): 3–7.

4. R. L. Piferi and K. A. Lawler, "Social Support and Ambulatory Blood Pressure: An Examination of Both Receiving and Giving," *International Journal of Psychophysiology* 62, no. 2 (2006): 328–336.

5. M. J. Poulin, S. L. Brown, A. J. Dillard, and D. M. Smith, "Giving to Others and the Association Between Stress and Mortality," *American Journal of Public Health* 103, no. 9 (2013): 1649–1655.

6. S. Q. Park, T. Kahnt, A. Dogan, S. Strang, E. Fehr, and P. N. Tobler, "A Neural Link Between Generosity and Happiness," *Nature Communications* 8 (2017): 15964.

7. E. W. Dunn, L. B. Aknin, and M. I. Norton, "Spending Money on Others Promotes Happiness," *Science* 319, no. 5870 (2008): 1687–1688.

Chapter 4: Say What's True

1. K. B. Serota, T. R. Levine, and F. J. Boster, "The Prevalence of Lying in America: Three Studies of Self-Reported Lies," *Human Communication Research* 36, no. 1 (2010): 2–25.

2. R. S. Feldman, J. A. Forrest, and B. R. Happ, "Self-Presentation and Verbal Deception: Do Self-Presenters Lie More?" *Basic and Applied Social Psychology* 24, no. 2 (2002): 163–170.

3. C. Connley, "More Than a Quarter of Professionals Under 40 Lie on Their Resume—Here's Why," CNBC, November 22, 2017, www.cnbc.com/2017/11/22/why-more-than-a-quarter-of-professionals-under-40-lie-on-their-resume.html.

4. N. Ellison, R. Heino, and J. Gibbs, "Managing Impressions Online: Self-Presentation Processes in the Online Dating Environment," *Journal of Computer-Mediated Communication* 11, no. 2 (2006): 415–441.

5. G. Kessler and M. Kelly, "President Trump Made 2,140 False or Misleading Claims in His First Year," *Washington Post*, January 20, 2018, www.washingtonpost.com/news/fact-checker/wp/2018/01/20/president-trump-made-2140-false-or-misleading-claims-in-his-first-year/?noredirect=on&utm_term=.fb07b8d9c226.

6. A. E. Kelly and L. Wang, "A Life Without Lies: Can Living More Honestly Improve Health?" Presentation to the American Psychological Association Annual Conven-

tion, August 2–5, 2012, https://cbsphilly.files.wordpress
.com/2012/08/kelly-a-life-without-lies.pdf.

7. B. Arcimowicz, K. Cantarero, and E. Soroko, "Motiva-
tion and Consequences of Lying: A Qualitative Analysis
of Everyday Lying," *Forum Qualitative Sozialforschung/
Forum: Qualitative Social Research* 16, no. 3 (September
2015).

8. L. Thompson, "Negotiation Tips: Lies, Damned Lies, and
Negotiations," Northwestern Kellogg website, 2014, www
.kellogg.northwestern.edu/news_articles/2014/05122014-
negotiation_lies.aspx.

Chapter 5: Make Sex Good

1. "What Consent Looks Like," RAINN, accessed May 29,
2019, www.rainn.org/articles/what-is-consent.

2. P. A. Levine, *Walking the Tiger: Healing Trauma* (Berke-
ley, CA: North Atlantic Books, 1997).

Chapter 6: Stay Clear

1. R. R. Griffiths, M. W. Johnson, M. A. Carducci, A. Um-
bricht, W. A. Richards, B. D. Richards, M. P. Cosimano,
and M. A. Klinedinst, "Psilocybin Produces Substantial
and Sustained Decreases in Depression and Anxiety in
Patients with Life-Threatening Cancer: A Randomized
Double-Blind Trial," *Journal of Psychopharmacology* 30,
no. 12 (2016): 1181–1197.

2. P. O. Johansen and T. S. Krebs, "Psychedelics Not Linked
to Mental Health Problems or Suicidal Behavior: A

RESOURCES

Books

Altered Traits: Science Reveals How Meditation Changes Your Mind, Brain, and Body by Daniel Goleman and Richard J. Davidson

American Dharma: Buddhism Beyond Modernity by Ann Gleig

Awakening Together: The Spiritual Practice of Inclusivity and Community by Larry Yang

In Love with the World: A Monk's Journey Through the Bardos of Living and Dying by Yongey Mingyur Rinpoche and Helen Tworkov

The Inner Work of Racial Justice: Healing Ourselves and Transforming Our Communities Through Mindfulness by Rhonda V. Magee

The Joy of Living: Unlocking the Secret and Science of Happiness by Yongey Mingyur Rinpoche and Eric Swanson

Lovingkindness: The Revolutionary Art of Happiness by Sharon Salzberg

Mindful of Race: Transforming Racism from the Inside Out by Ruth King

Mindfulness: A Practical Guide to Awakening by Joseph Goldstein

Radical Acceptance: Embracing Your Life with the Heart of a Buddha by Tara Brach

Radical Dharma: Talking Race, Love, and Liberation by Rev. angel Kyodo williams, Lama Rod Owens, and Jasmine Syedullah, PhD

Urban Tantra, Second Edition: Sacred Sex for the Twenty-First Century by Barbara Carrellas

When Awareness Becomes Natural: A Guide to Cultivating Mindfulness in Everyday Life by Sayadaw U Tejaniya

When Things Fall Apart: Heart Advice for Difficult Times by Pema Chödrön

Wherever You Go, There You Are: Mindfulness Meditation in Everyday Life by Jon Kabat-Zinn

Apps

10% Happier
Calm
Headspace
Insight Timer
Simple Habit

Organizations

Insight Meditation Society (dharma.org)
Spirit Rock Meditation Community (spiritrock.org)
Tergar Meditation Community (tergar.org)

INDEX OF MEDITATIONS

ABOUT THE AUTHORS

Craig and Devon Hase teach meditation workshops and retreats throughout North America and Europe. Devon is a mentor in Jack Kornfield and Tara Brach's Mindfulness Meditation Teacher Certification Program and teaches at Insight Meditation Society and Spirit Rock Meditation Center. Craig holds a PhD in counseling psychology, works as a therapist and coach, and teaches on the online platform Simple Habit. To learn more, visit www.satimindfulness.com.